THE YEAR

IN TENNIS 2005

Text by Chris Bowers

The International Tennis Federation

Universe

First published in the United States of America in 2006 by
UNIVERSE PUBLISHING A Division of Rizzoli International Publications, Inc.
300 Park Avenue South, New York, NY 10010
www.rizzoliusa.com

2006 2007 2008 / 10 9 8 7 6 5 4 3 2 1

Designed by Domino 4 Limited, Weybridge, Surrey
Printed in Italy

ISBN: 0-7893-1376-6
ISBN 13: 9 780789313768

CONTENTS

4 President's message

6 Foreword by Goran Ivanisevic

8 Introduction

12 First round

44 Photo feature: Better on the bench?

46 Player of the first round: Ivan Ljubicic

48 Quarterfinals

64 Photo feature: Cup colors

66 Player of the Quarterfinals: David Nalbandian

68 Semifinals

80 Photo feature: Theaters of dreams

82 Player of the Semifinals: Dominik Hrbaty

84 Play-off ties

100 Photo feature: See and be seen

102 Player of the Play-offs: Rafael Nadal

104 The Final

116 Photo feature: Outside the lines

118 Player of the Year: Ivan Ljubicic

120 Results

128 Acknowledgments and photography credits

PRESIDENT'S MESSAGE

IF PROOF WERE NEEDED that the Davis Cup by BNP Paribas is an event that is unique in tennis, then the 2005 edition of this competition provided it in glorious detail. This year also demonstrated that our great sport continues to grow around the world and that new powers are continually emerging in the modern game.

As Chris Bowers writes in the pages that follow, this year's Davis Cup by BNP Paribas was very much a product of tennis's reinstatement as an Olympic Sport as well as the tumultuous upheavals in Eastern Europe between 1989 and 1993. Both of these events opened tennis to a host of new markets and, in the Final this year, we could see the result of that.

In contrast to the more than 27,000 fans who packed the Estadio Olimpico de la Cartuja in Seville for the 2004 extravaganza between Spain and USA, this year's Final saw 4,100 spectators gather in the National Tennis Center in Bratislava to watch the Slovak Republic take on Croatia. For both of these young nations, it was a chance to show just how far they had come, in tennis terms and beyond, since their birth in the early 1990s.

One hundred and five years after USA defeated the British Isles 3–0 in the first-ever Davis Cup contest at the Longwood Cricket Club in Boston, the 2005 Final highlighted that the competition has also come an awful long way in its eventful history. And yet it also showed that it has stayed true to the ideals on which Dwight Davis founded it—fostering competition, respect, and a love for tennis right around the world.

Of course, Davis Cup by BNP Paribas is about more than just the Final. The Slovak Republic and Croatia were just two of a total of 130 nations that took part in the 2005 Davis Cup, which remains the largest annual international team competition in sport. With the World Group featuring the leading sixteen nations, the other teams contest one of three regional zones—Europe/Africa, Americas, and Asia/Oceania—in which winning promotion can be as important as capturing the Davis Cup trophy itself.

As ever, the game's leading players showed their passion and commitment for the competition despite the demands of the tennis calendar. In 2005, all of the world's Top 20 players made themselves available, with 62 of the Top 100 stepping onto court for their nations.

I would like to congratulate Ivan Ljubicic for his tremendous achievement in winning eleven live rubbers throughout the year, and of course Croatia for its success in becoming only the twelfth nation to win the Davis Cup by BNP Paribas. Its place at the top of the ITF Davis Cup Nations Ranking is richly deserved.

I will also look back with fondness at many other highlights of the year. The Slovak Republic enjoyed a thrilling run to the Final; Argentina, led superbly by David Nalbandian, pulled off a shock win over Australia on grass in Sydney; Andrei Pavel realized his dream of leading Romania to a quarterfinal; and Switzerland and the Netherlands fought out an incredible first-round clash. It was also pleasing to see Andre Agassi, such a great servant to the Davis Cup by BNP Paribas over the years, back in action for the USA.

For the second time, Chris Bowers has crafted a book that looks in detail at all twenty-three World Group and Play-off ties in the year. His extensive research, passion for the competition, and interviews with the participants ensure that the book is truly the story of how the Davis Cup by BNP Paribas year unfolded. Once again we are indebted to the world's leading tennis photographers, whose pictures provide a fitting complement to Chris's text.

Thank you to all 130 nations and 542 competitors that contested the Davis Cup by BNP Paribas in 2005. Their performances attracted the attention of millions of spectators, TV viewers, and internet users. To everyone who will take part in 2006, Good Luck!

Francesco Ricci Bitti
President, International Tennis Federation

FOREWORD

FIRST, I HAVE TO say that I never thought that I would find myself as a part of a Davis Cup championship team. It was a dream, of course. When you play for your country as many years as I did, you wonder if there is a chance that you might lift the beautiful silver Cup but realistically I found it hard to believe that a small country like mine would ever be the champion nation.

When we looked at the draw for 2005, having qualified for the World Group by defeating Belgium in the Play-offs, the obstacle ahead of us was to play away to the United States in the first round. And not just any US team but a team to which Andre Agassi had returned after a long absence from Davis Cup. Our chances didn't look very good but we got lucky. Always a good player, Ljubicic suddenly was a great player. He beat both Andre and Andy Roddick and then when he and Mario defeated the previously unbeaten Bryans, we were on our way.

The Quarterfinals and the Semis were at home in Croatia, a lot of fun but a lot of pressure for the whole team. Even though I wasn't playing, I was with the team the whole time and really felt a part of it. And Ljubicic continued to win. Three points against USA, three points against Romania, three points against Russia...unbelievable. I knew I was a good Davis Cup player and I had played against great Davis Cup players but I never saw anything like this.

The entire country was Davis Cup crazy after the Semifinals and, even though we played away to Slovak Republic, we felt we had a good chance to win. Their favorite surface is our favorite surface so that gave us confidence but never over-confidence. Dominik Hrbaty is an unbelievable player when he plays for his country and is always dangerous.

The end of the season was great for Croatia with Ivan playing in two Masters Series Finals and qualifying for the Masters, but, even with all that success, the one we all really wanted was the Davis Cup.

Even though Niki chose me for the team and even though I practiced like crazy to be ready, I knew it was unlikely that I would play. But, as hard as it was to sit on the sidelines, it was an honour that I will never forget. To watch Ivan and Mario play so well, to be part of the team, to hear the crowd singing and shouting, to feel the tension and then the joy of winning made this weekend possibly the most wonderful of my career, after winning Wimbledon.

I will remember the moment of victory, the moment when we were presented with the mini replicas, the moment we received the famous Davis Cup itself and our reception by 100,000 fans back home in Zagreb for the rest of my life. I may never be a player on a Croatian Davis Cup team again, but I think the players that we have could win many more and I hope one day to be their captain.

Goran Ivanisevic

Pictured opposite:

Goran Ivanisevic with his 2005 winner's trophy, alongside his father Srdjan

INTRODUCTION

IT WAS SO SHOCKING that many people couldn't bear to watch and turned off their televisions. In the early 1990s news bulletins around the world were dominated by images from the Yugoslav civil war, occasionally heart-rending, more often horrific, as the uneasy alliance of six states that had been Yugoslavia since 1918 descended into the brutality of neighbor-versus-neighbor civil war.

Towns that had once been known only to locals and the hardiest of tourists suddenly became globally recognized buzzwords for the conflict. Srebrenica, Mostar, Dubrovnik, Vukovar, Pristina. And Banja Luka. There, in 1992, as the tensions that were to lead to bombings, bloodshed, and the desecration of religious shrines just a few months later in the battle for control of Bosnia, a father tried to drive his restless twelve-year-old son to his tennis practice. They encountered a roadblock, with militia pointing guns at them. There was no choice but to go back. The man and his wife, both ethnic Croats, decided to get themselves and their family out of the impending bloodbath in the hope of finding a safer environment. But the only way of doing so was for the mother to take her two boys alone, and hope her husband would one day be able to follow. The man's name was Marko Ljubicic; his wife, Hazira; their sons, Vladan and Ivan. One spring day in 1992, Hazira, Vladan, and Ivan left on a bus that had to negotiate several barricades before reaching the airport. That day a seed was sown for the remarkable Davis Cup by BNP Paribas year of 2005.

The following year, a few hundred kilometers to the north, another seed was sown. The momentous upheavals in the governance of central and eastern Europe—that had begun with Hungary's decision to open its border with Austria in August 1989 and included the fall of the Berlin Wall, the collapse of the Soviet Union, and the Yugoslav civil war— featured one of the smoother handovers of power.

Like Yugoslavia, Czechoslovakia had existed since 1918, a federation of two Slav peoples who had fought together for their independence from the Austro-Hungarian empire. On January 1, 1993 the two split in an amicable divorce, but there was only room for one of them in the Davis Cup World Group. The International Tennis Federation gave Czechoslovakia's place to the Czech Republic as it clearly had the better players at the time. The new Slovak Republic therefore had to start from the bottom of the Davis Cup ladder, at times playing against nations with minimal tennis facilities. That sowed a seed of determination that came to fruition in 2005.

The third seed of the 2005 Davis Cup by BNP Paribas was sown more than a decade earlier. When the ITF president Philippe Chatrier embarked on his quest to have tennis reinstated as a full Olympic sport, his calculation was simple. If tennis was to survive in an increasingly competitive global sporting marketplace, it had to grow; if it was to grow it needed money; and that money would be much more easily forthcoming from governments if tennis were an Olympic sport. Chatrier's vision became a reality when tennis was reinstated after a sixty-four-year absence. By the time Steffi Graf and Miloslav Mecir won the gold medals at the Seoul Olympics of 1988, government money was flowing into tennis in numerous countries. It would only be a matter of time before the global tennis map would change.

In 2005 that change took effect. To the tennis purists it was shocking! The four Grand Slam nations and other Davis Cup powerhouses such as Sweden and Spain all failed to reach the Semifinals. The 2004 finalists, Spain and the USA, were eliminated in the first round. That seemed to open up the way for France and Australia, but they lost in the

Quarterfinals. If there was to be a new champion nation, it looked most likely to be Argentina, whose dominance of the men's world rankings finally seemed set to be reflected in the Davis Cup under the calming new captaincy of Alberto Mancini. Yet after conquering their aversion to away ties so spectacularly on the grass of Sydney, that away-tie hoodoo returned to haunt the South Americans on a rubberized hard court in Bratislava.

So the Davis Cup by BNP Paribas roll of honor and landscape was redrawn by the Slovak Republic and Croatia. For the first time in the twenty-fifth year of the World Group, two unseeded nations reached the Final.

The Slovaks had built a new National Tennis Center three years earlier, symbolically nestling between the country's national soccer and ice hockey stadiums on the northern edge of the capital, Bratislava. The symbolism lay in the fact that football and ice hockey were the Slovak Republic's premier sporting passions, but the two existing stadiums were aging and had been built in a bygone era. By contrast, the National Tennis Center was a new, state-of-the-art facility with a retractable roof. All that Slovak tennis needed now was a team to get the pulses of the nation's sports fans racing. The Slovak Republic's tennis players, led by the understated but passionate Dominik Hrbaty, provided that in 2005. As Hrbaty munched through several bowls of pasta in the on-site hotel his family helped invest in, could he possibly have been aware of the legacy he was building for his still only thirteen-year-old country?

Only a year older as a sovereign state, Croatia was also passionate about football—its team's run to the semifinals of the 1998 soccer World Cup was one of the highlights of its short national history. The other highlight was Goran Ivanisevic's unlikely Wimbledon triumph in 2001, which raised such emotions in Croatia that the whole of the country seemed to have turned out to greet him when he sailed into Split harbor on his return from London. To that extent the Croats were ahead of the Slovaks in their tennis development, and that may have had a slight influence on the destination of the Davis Cup.

Yet the prospect of Croatia and the Slovak Republic dominating the Davis Cup by BNP Paribas seemed a pipedream at the start of the year. This was supposed to be America's year, certainly from the point when the team that reached the 2004 Final was bolstered by the ageless Andre Agassi, persuaded out of Davis Cup retirement by the team spirit Patrick McEnroe had done so much to engender. And Spain were the team to beat after their triumph in 2004, as a new generation of Nadal, Lopez, and Verdasco got set to take over from Moya, Corretja and, Ferrero, and make Spain a nation for all surfaces and not just clay.

It might also have been Switzerland's year. Though he wouldn't admit it, perhaps Roger Federer regrets not playing his country's first-round tie against the Netherlands. A hitherto loyal servant of the team competition, he put the defense of his No. 1 ranking ahead of Davis Cup for 2005, only to find it was the year Switzerland discovered a second player in Stanislas Wawrinka. By the time Wawrinka had established himself in the top 100, Switzerland had lost to the Netherlands, and Federer returned for the damage-limitation exercise of a Play-off tie rather than the glory of a quarterfinal or semifinal.

That it didn't work out for any of the fancied names was but the latest sign of how team tennis defies the laws of that inexact science, expectation. It confirmed once again that when a player carries the passion and responsibility of representing something greater than just himself, rankings can go out the window. To those who merely follow the results of tennis, it must have seemed an odd year in which none of the fashionable teams did particularly well. But to those who delight in the ebb and flow of Davis Cup fortunes, it was a very special year.

This is the story of it. ●

first round 4–6 MARCH

Slovak Republic defeated Spain 4–1   BRATISLAVA, SLOVAK REPUBLIC—INDOOR HARD

Netherlands defeated Switzerland 3–2   FRIBOURG, SWITZERLAND—INDOOR HARD

Australia defeated Austria 5–0   SYDNEY, AUSTRALIA—OUTDOOR GRASS

Argentina defeated Czech Republic 5–0   BUENOS AIRES, ARGENTINA—OUTDOOR CLAY

Russia defeated Chile 4–1   MOSCOW, RUSSIA—INDOOR CARPET

France defeated Sweden 3–2   STRASBOURG, FRANCE—INDOOR CLAY

Romania defeated Belarus 3–2   BRASOV, ROMANIA—INDOOR CLAY

Croatia defeated USA 3–2   CARSON, CA, USA—OUTDOOR HARD

FIRST ROUND

IN SOME WAYS, THE 2005 Davis Cup by BNP Paribas began in October 2004. It had certainly begun by January 20, 2005.

Facing Spain on a slow clay court in Seville, the American captain Patrick McEnroe approached Andre Agassi, the 1999 French Open champion, asking him if he would come out of Davis Cup retirement for the 2004 Final. Agassi had quit the team competition after the USA's 5–0 defeat to Spain in the 2000 Semifinals—he wasn't on that team; in fact, his absence contributed to the defeat that led to John McEnroe's resignation as American captain. But with Patrick McEnroe ushering in a new era for U.S. tennis, Agassi decided his time playing for his country had come and gone as a new generation took over.

That perhaps explains why Agassi initially declined to join the young guns, which the younger McEnroe had molded from a group of promising rookies into America's first finalists since 1997. He explained his philosophy was "all or nothing," and he didn't want to jump aboard the U.S. bandwagon just for the glory of the Final.

But the mainstays of that U.S. team—Andy Roddick and the doubles team of Mike and Bob Bryan—let Agassi know that he would not only be welcomed back into the fold, but they would positively relish being a teammate of someone they had idolized when they were growing up. After beating Rainer Schuettler in the second round of the Australian Open, Agassi said: "I'm going to have a discussion with Patrick. I had a lot of regret not playing because Davis Cup is one of the best memories of my career. To experience playing with another generation of guys that have such a good fellowship and team camaraderie would be a great feeling."

Though nothing could be confirmed, the possibility of Andre Agassi revoking his decision to retire and joining the U.S. team for 2005 was at least alive.

McEnroe finally had his chat with Agassi a week after the American's straight-sets defeat to Roger Federer in the Australian Open quarterfinals. He made it clear that Agassi would not be expected to commit for a full year, thereby removing the 34-year-old's need for "all or nothing." Agassi was clearly tempted but felt he wanted to be sure the team wanted him. So he sent McEnroe home, and phoned Roddick and the Bryans. He then took time to chat to his wife, Steffi Graf, and have a night to sleep on it. The following day he phoned McEnroe to say he was in.

"I wasn't getting too much sleep because I was hoping to get that call," recalled McEnroe in the run-up to the first round against Croatia, "so I was extremely excited when he told me he was looking to come back. It's our guys on the team that deserve the credit for getting him back, because without their attitudes and passion I'm not sure that Andre would be here today."

"I think that when you get older your capacity to embrace special moments grows," Agassi said on the Tuesday of the first round tie. "I certainly feel that way this week. I've been away from my family for ten days, and coming here, I even requested from the home front a few extra days to be able to enjoy being around the guys and get to know them better. That speaks for my enthusiasm about this environment and how much I've missed it. It's something I'm really looking forward to and I hope it's not the last time."

The build-up to the first round had centered around one man. And indeed the weekend did center around one man. But it was not to be Agassi. ●

Pictured on previous page:

Guillermo Canas (ARG), whose contribution to Argentina's defeat of the Czech Republic was a high point of a year in which he was subsequently found guilty of a doping offense

Pictured from top:

Andre Agassi (USA); Patrick McEnroe (Captain, USA);

The US team lines up in Carson (l to r: Andy Roddick, Andre Agassi, Bob and Mike Bryan, Captain Patrick McEnroe)

USA v **CROATIA**

IVAN LJUBICIC ARRIVED IN Carson, a municipality between central Los Angeles and the Pacific coast cities at Long Beach, as one of the form players of the year. Though he had lost in the second round of the Australian Open to Marcos Baghdatis, he had reached four finals in the first eight weeks of 2005. OK, so he had lost them all, but three were to the runaway world No. 1 Roger Federer, two of them in three sets, one on a final-set tiebreak.

That led to two schools of thought. Either this was the second-best player of the year behind the phenomenal Swiss, or it was a guy running into form and making use of some moderately favorable draws. The three days in Carson suggested that Ljubicic, if not world No. 2, was playing tennis worthy of the top five. But few suspected that as the American team sat down for its post-draw news conference. The amount of tennis he had played, allied to the fact that he would have to play on all three days, suggested the threat he posed would be enough for Agassi and Roddick to handle.

Agassi had been drawn to face Ljubicic in the opening rubber, full of the joys of being back in the Davis Cup fold. He was happy to accept that he was up against a formidable first-day opponent, but he gave a revealing, if perhaps unwitting, insight into the American team's confidence. Asked whether he had overcome his aversion to playing dead rubbers, Agassi replied: "The issue of a dead rubber is a bit like taxes: it's just a good problem to have. I hope we have the painful conversation of whether me or any of us are going to be playing on Sunday. But that would be great news."

In other words, the only reason there could be a dead rubber would be if the U.S. had won. No consideration was given to the possibility that Croatia could win in four, or even three rubbers. Were the Americans taking Croatia too lightly after all?

In gusting conditions, Agassi was finding it hard to find the middle of his strings as he and Ljubicic warmed up for the first action of the weekend. When he dropped his opening service game, the 34-year-old could easily have put it down to a sleepy start, and when he broke back for 3–4, he seemed finally to be into the match. But he was broken the following game as Ljubicic won the first set.

When Ljubicic had break points early in the second, alarm bells were starting to ring. But then Agassi went for more variety and was suddenly 5–2 up. He was now surely into his stride.

Only he wasn't. He clearly had a game plan of hitting as much as possible to Ljubicic's backhand, but the Croat's clever use of heavy topspin mixed with severe slice forced Agassi to alternate between playing high balls outside his comfort zone and generating his own pace. He was also being taken wide by Ljubicic's viciously kicking serve to the advantage court. It meant he had little margin for error, and when he dropped serve for 5–4, it was to prove the most costly missed opportunity of the match, perhaps the entire weekend. Ljubicic held two more service games to take the set into the tiebreak, and then played faultless tennis to take it 7–0.

Agassi's best hope of turning the match around seemed to lie in tapping into a new vein of intensity, and serving at 2–3 in the third set it was almost handed to him. Umpire Lars Graff overruled an "out" call on Agassi's baseline, which Agassi accepted, but he was then horrified to find Graff had given the point to Ljubicic rather than asking it to be replayed. Agassi was furious and promptly dropped serve.

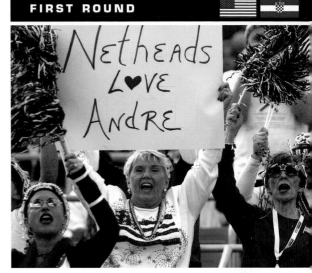

Pictured from top:

American fans welcome Agassi back to Davis Cup; Croatian fans turned out in force; Andre Agassi (USA) and Ivan Ljubicic (CRO)

USA v **CROATIA** CONTINUED

The anger gave him plenty of fire, and he had three break-back points at 2–4 and another at 3–5. But Ljubicic was not going to let his man off the hook, and ran out the victor 6–3 7–6(0) 6–3 in two hours and six minutes.

Oh, the irony! The Achilles heel of the U.S. team in 2004 had seemed to be the lack of a second singles player to back up Roddick. Agassi's presence was supposed to fill that void, but here was Roddick with all the pressure again, needing to win his singles against Mario Ancic, another man in form having been in the Scottsdale final the weekend before.

And it couldn't have got off to a worse start for the American. Two double faults in the opening game handed Ancic the break, and while Roddick got back to 2–2, he conceded again for 2–3, a break he was not to recover. The pattern was almost identical to the first set of Agassi v Ljubicic.

But Roddick broke the pattern. He held to love at the start of the second set and broke Ancic in the fourth game. The set was his, and so, in effect, was the contest. He broke another four times, most crucially in the first game of the fourth set, thwarting a mini-revival by the Croat. Roddick's 4–6 6–2 6–1 6–4 win left the tie level after the opening day.

If there was one "banker" point for the Americans, it was thought to be the doubles. The identical twins, Mike and Bob Bryan, natives of southern California for whom this was very much a home tie, took into the match against Ljubicic and Ancic not just an unbeaten 5–0 Davis Cup record, but they had never dropped a set. Many of those 15 sets had been against lesser opposition than the 2004 Olympic bronze medalists, but when the twins took the first set thanks to a break of Ancic's first service game, there seemed a gulf in class.

But it all turned around in the second-set tiebreak. Both Ljubicic and Ancic picked up their level in the middle of the set. Ljubicic said later when asked what difference his Olympic bronze medal had made to his doubles confidence: "That changed my career, and not only in doubles. Since then I've played really great tennis. I haven't played a lot of doubles after the Olympic medal, but after a set and a half I started to play better, return better, volley better, and everything was coming up."

The set went into a dramatic tiebreak, which perhaps determined the whole tie. The Bryans had three set points, one of them on their own serve. The Croats had three more set points (they had had one at 5–4), none on their own serve, but when a Ljubicic backhand went down the line at 9–8 for a winner, the Bryans' sequence had finally been broken.

"That tiebreak was very, very important," said Croatia's captain, Niki Pilic. "With that we really got our game up."

Mike Bryan said: "That set point we had when we were serving, that in our mind was kind of a match point, because we're pretty good frontrunners: when we get a lead we never look back. I think we didn't stick a couple of volleys, and they got better as the match went on. They never got tight, I don't think they ever missed two or three first serves in a row, which is pretty tough."

The Bryans might have turned the match back in their favor had they won the marathon third game of the third set, but on a day when the right-handed twin's serve—usually weaker than leftie Bob's—seemed especially weak, the break went Croatia's way, and the visitors ran out winners 3–6 7–6(8) 6–4 6–4.

Pictured from top:

Croatia takes charge of the doubles rubber;

Ivan Ljubicic (CRO); Andy Roddick (USA)

Pictured opposite:

Andre Agassi (USA)

That kept alive the prospect of a fairy-tale finish. With Ljubicic admitting to tiredness, Roddick was favorite to beat him in the first reverse singles, and surely Agassi would not miss his chance of glory in a live fifth. Yet by Saturday night Ljubicic had gone five Davis Cup matches unbeaten against Americans, including his three wins in Croatia's triumph over the USA in Zagreb in 2003. Who would bet against him in this form?

In front of the first truly vocal crowd of the weekend, Roddick started more adventurously. He attacked Ljubicic and broke in the fifth game, going on to win the set. As the second set neared its conclusion, Ljubicic seemed to be showing signs of tiredness. But then Roddick played four bad points from 40–15 up, Ljubicic broke for 5–3, and suddenly it was one set all.

The pair traded breaks in the third set, so another tiebreak would prove crucial. The Americans were enjoying it when Roddick opened up a 4–1 lead in the tiebreak, but Ljubicic then won the next four points. By the time they got to 11–11, each player had missed three set points. Then at 12–11 Roddick put an in-to-out forehand just into the tramlines, and the set was Ljubicic's.

With Ljubicic just a set away from a magnificent victory, Roddick kept piling on the pressure. If he was guilty of anything, it was going for too much on a day when his groundstrokes—especially the forehand—lacked consistency and his opponent's gas tank might have been close to empty. But he worked his opportunities. He had two break points at 2–2 and opened up a 6–3 lead in the fourth set tiebreak. He persisted in making life difficult for himself, squandering all three set points and then a fourth at 7–6, before watching in relief as Ljubicic double faulted at 8–7.

"I felt great going into the fifth set," he said. "I knew I still had my legs under me and that he was dogging on some balls late in the fourth."

But at the turning point Roddick had worked so hard for, the match failed to turn. It was Ljubicic who seemed to find new energy: "Today I felt really good," he said later. "I could go forever, I had the feeling. My knee was bothering me in the beginning of the fifth, but physically I felt like the muscles were pretty good."

A tired-looking Roddick was broken to love in the opening game of the fifth set. He had three break-back points at 2–1, but when Ljubicic saved them all and then broke for 4–1, Roddick was left with too much work to do. At 4–1 Ljubicic needed treatment for his knee—a mild recurrence of an existing problem—but as Roddick observed wryly afterward: "Unfortunately for me he can still serve 135 [miles per hour] while getting treated."

The moment of victory brings mixed reactions, but when Ljubicic completed his remarkable weekend by winning 4–6 6–3 7–6(11) 6–7(7) 6–2 in two minutes under four hours, he just spread his arms wide and smiled beatifically to the darkening Californian skies.

That smile summed up the likeable Croat, who had waited several years for his immense talent to flower. It wasn't just his weight of shot, his astute use of the court, and his physical endurance that saw him to three victories over one of the best teams ever to be paraded in the Davis Cup by BNP Paribas. What counted for more was his calmness under pressure, his unwillingness to be fazed by a passionate final-day crowd, and his ability to think his way through a match against a man who had beaten him the previous five times they had played.

Pictured from top:

Andy Roddick (USA); Croatian team celebrates

Pictured opposite:

Mario Ancic congratulates Ivan Ljubicic

USA v **CROATIA** CONTINUED

Asked how the win would go down in Croatia, Ljubicic said: "I imagine it's going to be huge, but not only at home, I think all around the world. It's big news to beat Andre, the Bryans, and Roddick in three days. It's amazing."

"Amazing" was probably a word the Americans would also have used to sum up the weekend, but with a very different emphasis. For them it was the first-ever defeat in a first round tie at home, and it made the debut of the "dream team" something of a nightmare. Little wonder Agassi's aversion to dead rubbers returned, leaving Bob Bryan to post a three-sets victory over Croatia's Roko Karanusic. ●

ROMANIA v BELARUS

FEW PEOPLE IN CARSON, California, had heard of Brasov, Romania, but the mountainous city that hosts more ski tourists than tennis fans held a constant fascination during the first-round weekend. For if Romania beat Belarus, the USA would be at home in the quarterfinals, whereas if Belarus had won, the U.S. would have to travel.

All this, of course, assumed that the Americans would beat Croatia. By the end of the weekend the U.S. had its wish from Brasov—a Romanian victory—but Ivan Ljubicic's heroics rendered Romania's victory irrelevant to the Americans.

If Ljubicic was Croatia's hero, Andrei Pavel was Romania's. For many years Pavel found himself in the position Roger Federer occupies in Switzerland—holding the fate of his country almost entirely in his own hands. This was his fifth Davis Cup by BNP Paribas World Group First Round tie, and he had yet to make it to the quarterfinals. But now it was to be his moment.

Not since 1983 had Romania been in the last eight, and that was with Ilie Nastase still playing. Pavel made his Davis Cup debut in 1991, and of his four previous first round ties, two had gone to live fifth rubbers. The first came in 1997 when Romania led the Dutch 2–0 after the first day but Pavel lost the decider to Paul Haarhuis; the second in 2001 when Pavel could only watch as his doubles partner, Gabriel Trifu, lost the decider to Germany's Nicolas Kiefer.

The choice of Brasov was based on the surface. All else being equal, Romania's top players, Pavel and Victor Hanescu, would probably have picked a quick court. But against Belarus's two-man team of Max Mirnyi and Vladimir Voltchkov, lovers of fast surfaces who had been semifinalists just six months earlier, the Romanians wanted clay. The Romanian weather in March meant it had to be indoors, and no clay options were available in Bucharest. So for the first time since 1988, Romania took a World Group tie outside its capital, to the 2,000-seat Popescu Colibasi Arena.

For their part, Belarus indulged in a little kidology, naming 17-year-old Aliaksandr Bury to partner Mirnyi in the doubles. No one expected Bury to play, and indeed he didn't—Vladimir Voltchkov said it was "just a tactical thing" after his singles on Friday—but it was a way for Belarus's new captain, Andrei Biassonau, to tell his opponents he had more than two players to choose from.

Pictured from top:

Andrei Pavel (ROM); Vladimir Voltchkov (BLR)

Pictured opposite:

Ivan Ljubicic (CRO)

Pictured from top:

Max Mirnyi (BLR); Victor Hanescu (ROM) is congratulated

by Romanian legend Ilie Nastase

Pictured opposite:

Victor Hanescu (ROM) is embraced by his captain, Florin Segarceanu

ROMANIA v BELARUS CONTINUED

Mirnyi increased his Davis Cup record to 38 wins in 55 matches with a 7–6(6) 6–4 3–6 6–4 win over Hanescu. The first-set tiebreak proved crucial, Hanescu squandering a 3–0 and 4–2 lead before losing it 8–6. Until then neither man had dropped serve, but from the start of the second, Hanescu started to look vulnerable, and though Mirnyi dropped the third, he never looked seriously threatened after the tiebreak.

It was important for Mirnyi and Pavel, who both had to play on all three days, to win as quickly as possible, and Pavel went one better than Mirnyi with his straight-sets victory over Vladimir Voltchkov. Not that any of the three sets was easy. It took until the tenth game for Pavel to break in the first set, and he needed two tiebreaks for a 6–4 7–6(2) 7–6(2) victory. The comfort Belarus took was that Voltchkov got better and better as the match wore on, so his confidence in the event of a live fifth rubber would be reasonably high.

Mirnyi and Voltchkov once again showed that their form in Davis Cup by BNP Paribas is so much better than on the regular tour. Teaming up for the 20th time, they posted their 15th win, beating Pavel and his long-time Davis Cup doubles partner, Gabriel Trifu, 7–6(3) 6–3 6–4. This was as one-sided as the score suggested and left Pavel distinctly demoralized.

"I was feeling the pressure of having to play well in all my three rubbers," he admitted several weeks later, the memory of that Saturday still vivid.

That night Pavel dined on his own, determined to get his head around the task of beating Mirnyi the following day. A devoted team player, he felt the best he could do for his side was to withdraw from his colleagues.

To the outside world that night, the Davis Cup prowess of a small nation once again looked like it would be causing an upset. Belarus was a province of the Soviet Union while Ion Tiriac and Ilie Nastase were playing out the golden age of Romanian tennis in the 1970s, and the power of its team spirit had the potential to overcome the resurgent Romania.

"I played together with Voltchkov many times in the past," said Mirnyi after the doubles, "and we understand each other almost perfectly. Besides, we felt huge support from our supporters and bench."

But Pavel's lone dinner did the trick. He played superbly in a first set that saw him outserve the powerful Mirnyi. Mirnyi broke at the start of the second but was broken back in the fifth game in what was probably the crucial section of the match. For while the set went to the tiebreak, the force was by then back with Pavel, and he won it without dropping a point.

Mirnyi bounced back to take the third, but he was broken crucially in the second game of the fourth set, and while he had chances to get the break back, he couldn't convert any of them. Pavel ran out a 6–1 7–6(0) 4–6 6–3 winner.

So for the third time, Pavel found his chances of a first Davis Cup Quarterfinal resting on a live fifth rubber. As against Germany in 2001, he had to rely on a teammate for his dream to come true, in this case Hanescu.

"I was confident about him," Pavel admitted later, "but pretty scared as well. Voltchkov can play amazing in Davis Cup."

ROMANIA v BELARUS CONTINUED

Pavel's fears seemed to be realized as Voltchkov broke early, but serving for the first set at 5–4, he was broken, as Hanescu got into the match. Once again a tiebreak—the sixth of the weekend and there was one in every rubber—proved crucial. Hanescu won it 7–2, and rode the momentum to break for a commanding lead in the second set, which he eventually took 6–4.

Yet few write off Voltchkov in Davis Cup until he is actually beaten. He has always been able to raise his game for Davis Cup, and he had won a live fifth rubber a year earlier when only half-fit against the mighty Russians. So when he opened up a 4–1 lead in the tiebreak, a nervous fourth set for the home faithful was on the cards. But Hanescu clawed back the deficit, and at 7–6 he hit an ace, which finally gave Pavel his first Davis Cup Quarterfinal.

"It was really a dream come true," Pavel said. "After the dream team of the 1970s with Nastase and Tiriac, we had waited 22 years. I love Davis Cup, the team spirit, and when you win a good point in a home tie and the crowd starts chanting your name, it's amazing. We had done so much playing to get into the World Group, and then playing to stay in the World Group and then get back into the World Group again, and finally we were in the quarterfinals. It was amazing, we were so happy, we jumped onto the court and the champagne was flowing. I had waited so long, too long really, but it's better late than never." ●

SLOVAK REPUBLIC
v SPAIN

HOW FAST IS FAST? This question, combining physics with philosophy, was exercising the minds of those at Slovakic Republic's new National Tennis Center in Bratislava in the run-up to Spain's first defense of its 2004 title.

Expecting to field a team of Dominik Hrbaty, Karol Beck, Karol Kucera, and Michal Mertinak (Kucera ultimately didn't play because of injury), the Slovaks were always going to opt for any surface other than clay against the nation that picks clay for every home tie. But in choosing Premier hard, it went for a surface that was faster than grass. That's fast. Very fast.

Unfairly fast, said the Spaniards in their Tuesday news conference. They said they had always picked clay, but always fair clay, never artificially slow. They even said they were complaining to the ITF. The ITF had sent its President, Francesco Ricci Bitti, to the tie, not out of a telepathic sense of impending controversy, but because Ricci Bitti had heard so much about the impressive tennis center in Bratislava, opened just two years earlier, that he wanted to see it for himself. He pointed out that the surface in the 4,000-seater Sibamac Arena was quite within the rules pertaining to acceptable surfaces; in fact, the rules allowed for even faster surfaces.

And, as the old sporting cliché goes, it was the same for both sides. The Spaniards might legitimately have complained about the speed of the court potentially spoiling the spectacle, but there was no reason the Spanish team of 2005 should have feared a

Pictured opposite:

The National Tennis Center, Bratislava

Pictured from top:

Fernando Verdasco (ESP);

Spanish Captain Jordi Arrese with Feliciano Lopez

Pictured from top:

Karol Beck (SVK); Feliciano Lopez (ESP);

Rafael Nadal and Albert Costa (ESP)

Pictured opposite:

Dominik Hrbaty (SVK)

SLOVAK REPUBLIC v SPAIN CONTINUED

surface of such pace. After all, even in the absence of three of the four stalwarts of the 2004 Final-winning team—Carlos Moya, Juan Carlos Ferrero, and Tommy Robredo—they still had a formidable line-up.

Many teams would have been grateful to field Feliciano Lopez on such a fast court. Twice into the fourth round at Wimbledon, the 23-year-old from Toledo brought the ideal fast-court game to Bratislava, along with a world ranking of 21, and the experience of having won a pressure-laden fourth rubber against the Czech Tomas Berdych a year earlier to prevent Spanish hopes of a second title disappearing before the first 2004 World Group weekend was complete.

Many teams would likewise have been grateful to field Fernando Verdasco, who was viewed in 2004 and early 2005 as a genuinely exciting prospect in tennis. Like Lopez, the 21-year-old from Madrid was a big-serving left-hander, reared on clay, but not afraid to try his luck on faster courts.

And which team would not have been grateful for Rafael Nadal, the find of the 2004 Davis Cup by BNP Paribas? Though he was still a few weeks off his major breakthrough tournaments in Miami, Monte Carlo, Rome, and Roland Garros, he came to Bratislava in hot form, having won back-to-back titles in Costa do Sauipe and Acapulco.

Yet perhaps those two titles on slow clay, combined with the fast Premier hard court in Bratislava, fooled the Spaniards. With Nadal flying in from Mexico on the Tuesday of the tie, Spain's technical committee led by Jordi Arrese decided to rest him on the opening day to give him added time to acclimatize to the surface. They then put him into the doubles with the experienced Albert Costa, with a view to throwing him into a crucial singles on the final day. Nice idea, but by the final day, the tie was over—and the Slovaks hungover from celebrating.

The damage was really done in the opening rubber. Though the Sibamac Arena has a retractable roof, there was never any question of it being opened—temperatures outside were sub-zero, and fresh snow lay on the streets of the Slovak capital. The Slovak players' habit of wearing their national ice hockey team's shirts while supporting from the bench could have made it seem cold inside as well, but the atmosphere was red hot. In attendance were the Slovak Prime Minister, Mikulas Dzurinda; the Slovak President, Ivan Gasparovic; and 4,000 loudly cheering Slovak fans. The Slovak Republic had come to the ball game.

Feliciano Lopez had not. Though present in body, the Spanish No. 1 for the tie was absent in mind, and played one of the matches he said he would be "happy to forget." His opening service game was taken by Karol Beck, the 43rd-ranked Slovak No. 2, and while Lopez broke back en route to leveling at 4–4, he was broken again in the tenth game as Beck took the opening set.

The turning point for Lopez should have been the ninth game of the second, when he held three break points. Beck held serve, putting the pressure right back on Lopez. The Spaniard held for 5–5, but succumbed two games later as Beck broke to open a two-sets-to-love lead.

Lopez could be forgiven for trying something different, but his decision to stay back and put less trust in his net game played right into the solid Slovak's hands, and a break in the eighth game sufficed for a 6–4 7–5 6–3 win.

Pictured above:

The victorious Slovak team celebrates knocking out the holders

SLOVAK REPUBLIC v SPAIN CONTINUED

In one rubber, the energy of the whole tie had shifted. If the tie had started as the Slovak Republic having the chance of a shock win against the mighty Spaniards, it was now the home side that were favorites. Suddenly Fernando Verdasco was no longer one of the most promising players in world tennis, but a highly inexperienced player making his Davis Cup debut against the wily Dominik Hrbaty. The difference in rankings was a mere eight places—Hrbaty's 29th to Verdasco's 37th—but the momentum was Slovak.

The early break, which allowed Hrbaty to take the first set, seemed to be a continuation of Beck's match against Lopez. But Verdasco was entitled to some nerves, and by the end of the first set he was at least in the match, if a set adrift. In the second he opened up a 4–1 lead, only to see Hrbaty storm back to win five games on the run.

By now the atmosphere was like a soccer match, a vociferous but fair crowd relishing the sight of their players riding the crest of a wave, serenaded by a charismatic musician playing a number of instruments, notably drums. And when Hrbaty led the third-set tiebreak 5–2 he was just two points away from victory, but the feisty Verdasco came back to win it 9–7, giving Spain hope that it might salvage something from the first day.

When Verdasco broke in the opening game of the fourth set, a dramatic turnaround was on the cards. But Hrbaty broke straight back, and a second break for 5–3 ended Spanish resistance, the 27-year-old Slovak winning 6–3 6–4 6–7(7) 6–3.

If the massed ranks of Slovak fans were ecstatic, those with long memories were a little more cautious. In the first round of 1998, the Slovak Republic took a 2–0 lead over a depleted line-up from the then mighty Sweden, only to lose the next three rubbers, and the Slovak captain Miloslav Mecir was not letting anyone forget that on the Friday night: "I didn't expect to be leading 2–0," he said. "With the high quality of the Spanish players I was even a little worried that it could be the other way around. But we are completely aware that we need three points, and I haven't forgotten the tie against Sweden, so the work is far from being done."

Mecir was busy doing his own work on Friday night and Saturday morning. Figuring that neither side had a great doubles team, he felt his team's best chance to win lay with Hrbaty beating Lopez in the first reverse singles. He therefore opted to give Hrbaty a day's rest, and put Beck and Mertinak into the doubles for the first time in Davis Cup. It meant the Slovak pair had nothing to lose, while Spain's Nadal and Costa—also playing for the first time together in Davis Cup—had Spain's hard-won title to lose. It turned the doubles on its head and had the champagne flowing by late afternoon on Saturday.

All four players served well in the opening set, but the freely striking Beck and Mertinak dominated the tiebreak, winning it 7–3. That put added spice into their game, which allowed them to break Costa for 2–1 in the second set. It proved the only break of serve in the entire match, but Spain had two set points on the Beck serve in the tenth game of the third. As the set went into an almost inevitable tiebreak, the tension mounted. The Slovak Republic had a match point at 6–5 after leading 5–3. Spain had a

third set point at 7–6, and a fourth at 8–7, this time on their own serve. But the Slovaks saved it, and then had a second match point at 9–8, also on their own serve. This time Beck made no mistake, and the 7–6(3) 6–4 7–6(8) scoreline meant the champions were out at the first hurdle. History had repeated itself, just as the Spanish champions of 2000 went out in the first round—and inside two days—in 2001, that time against the Netherlands in Eindhoven.

Beck, who had started the week with a cold and cough, ended it as the Slovak hero. He was showered with champagne and tossed into the air by his teammates. For him, it was a first Davis Cup Quarterfinal, but for Hrbaty and Kucera it was a third. With the draw promising the Slovaks more home ties, Mecir was left to wonder if his still-young nation— it ceded from Czechoslovakia just 12 years earlier—would be "third-time lucky" in the last eight. ●

SWITZERLAND
v NETHERLANDS

THE SLOVAK REPUBLIC'S HEROICS meant the Sunday in Bratislava was not just a celebration over the dead rubbers, but a chance to keep up with play on a dramatic third day in Fribourg. For the winners of the Switzerland-Netherlands tie would have to travel to Bratislava for the quarterfinals.

Though the world No. 1, Roger Federer, had declared himself unavailable for this weekend, the tie proved so wildly exciting that Switzerland's captain Marc Rosset said: "In my 14 years in Davis Cup I have experienced a lot, but this was one of the best weeks. Our comradeship was great, and we have shown that alongside Roger we have other players. We've waited a long time for that."

The absence of the two biggest names—as well as Federer, the Netherlands' Martin Verkerk, the former Roland Garros finalist, was still recovering from shoulder surgery—did nothing to prevent three days of excitement and emotion. The most inexperienced Swiss team for at least 30 years—not one player in the world's top 100—put up a valiant effort to show it could still justify its World Group status even in the absence of its illustrious star. That it narrowly lost should take nothing away from a superb and dramatic weekend's tennis.

The sleepy town of Fribourg is one of Switzerland's lesser-known beauty spots. It sits on the linguistic borderline—known colloquially in Switzerland as the Rösti trench— between the French- and German-speaking parts of the quadrilingual country, and would be better known by its German name of Freiburg if there weren't another (and better known) Freiburg just across the border in southwestern Germany. Fribourg's Expo Arena had rigged up seating for just under 5,000 spectators, who saw seven and three-quarter hours of play on the opening day alone.

For Switzerland, the positive to take from defeat was the experience earned by its two singles players, Marco Chiudinelli and Stanislas Wawrinka, both of whom were

Pictured from top:

The Swiss and Dutch teams line up in Fribourg; Swiss fans were still out in force despite Roger Federer's absence; Peter Wessels (NED)

SWITZERLAND v **NETHERLANDS** CONTINUED

playing their first live Davis Cup rubbers. In the continuing absence of Michel Kratochvil, both had emerged as pretenders to be Roger Federer's back-up, Chiudinelli by finally knuckling down to do justice to the immense talent he had somewhat neglected, Wawrinka by building on a promising junior career that saw him win the Roland Garros boys' title in 2003.

The significance for the Dutch—apart from winning—was in blooding the 26-year-old Peter Wessels in his first Davis Cup tie, and allowing Sjeng Schalken to slowly rebuild his confidence after a year of the strength-sapping condition, mononucleosis.

Chiudinelli was particularly impressive in his 7–6(4) 4–6 6–3 5–7 6–2 defeat to Schalken in the opening rubber. In his first-ever best-of-five-sets match, he came back from 3–5 down in the fourth set to force a decider.

"In a normal tour event I wouldn't have won the fourth set," he said afterward. "It's like a dream to be on the court with such a fantastic crowd."

A lack of experience meant Chiudinelli dropped the first four games of the final set, and there was no way back after that, but Schalken was impressed with his opponent: "He's a good fighter, and I found no weaknesses in his game."

Schalken himself came through a difficult first two sets, when his back was "blocked," but after receiving treatment at the start of the third set, he relaxed, and apart from losing 16 of the last 17 points of the fourth set he was the better player in the crucial stages.

Despite the relatively slow Rebound Ace court laid by the Swiss to soak up some of the power of the big Dutch servers, Wawrinka and Wessels held serve as if it was a much faster court. Neither dropped serve until the final game of Wessels's 7–6(12) 6–7(4) 7–6(7) 6–4 win that gave the Netherlands a 2–0 lead after day one. The match was won more on nerve than anything else, the set point Wawrinka missed in the first tiebreak and the one he missed in the third proving very costly. Though he has a complete game, Wawrinka's nerves let him down at crucial stages in both his singles, whereas Wessels's nerve held firm.

With the big-serving Wessels having taken his chance to establish himself as a worthy Davis Cup player in the singles, he then found himself with a second chance in the doubles alongside Dennis van Scheppingen, as Raemon Sluiter had to pull out with a leg injury.

If seven and three-quarter hours was a long first-day total, by the end of day two the total was over twelve after a four-and-a half-hour doubles that the 4,000 spectators will never forget. Rosset brought George Bastl back to the Davis Cup fold to partner Federer's regular Davis Cup partner, Yves Allegro, and after a nervous start the two combined well to set up a thrilling climax.

Despite trying too hard early on, Allegro grew in confidence as the match progressed. He led a fight back from two-sets-to-love down, and his crisp volleying saved three match points for the home nation, one in the fourth set, and two in the fifth. When the Swiss broke to lead 7–6 in the decider, hopes were high and the crowd was crazy, but the Dutch broke back for 7–7. Again the Swiss broke, and this time Allegro served out the 5–7 4–6 7–6(5) 7–5 9–7 victory to put behind him a poor serving display that had included 17 double faults.

Pictured opposite:
Sjeng Schalken (NED)
Pictured from top:
Marco Chiudinelli (SUI); The Swiss bench

Pictured from top:
Stanislas Wawrinka (SUI); The Netherlands
team in high spirits after their victory

Forty-four times in Davis Cup, Switzerland had ended the first day 0–2 down. Not once had it come back to win the tie, but after the doubles, a remarkable result seemed plausible, especially as Wessels ended the match looking very tired and struggling with back problems. The belief in both camps was that the fourth rubber would take on the status of a fifth and decide the whole tie.

It was another thriller. Schalken eventually won it in one minute over four hours, after saving four match points.

Wawrinka stormed through the first set, but Schalken came back to take the second and third. Wawrinka regrouped to take the fourth and used that momentum to build up a 4–1 lead—with two breaks—in the fifth. Surely from this point he couldn't lose? But Schalken had played 33 Davis Cup rubbers, and that experience started to count as Wawrinka became increasingly nervous.

At 5–4 Wawrinka served for victory. At 30–15 he was the victim of a dubious call that would have given him two match points, much to his frustration. But the 19-year-old still worked up four match points. On the second both he and the home crowd were rejoicing after a line judge called out, but despite his later protestations the call was clearly wrong and the umpire Enric Molina instantly overruled. On the fourth match point, Wawrinka made a model approach to the net, only to see an astonishing sliced backhand passing shot played from well behind the baseline beat him.

When Schalken broke for 5–5 and then held for 6–5, the match looked over. But Wawrinka saved two match points before holding for 6–6. He then broke again for 7–6, but his tank was running on empty. Schalken won the next three games to see the Dutch through to another quarterfinal on a wide Wawrinka forehand that rather summed up the Swiss player's weekend—so near and yet so far.

The fact that Wessels retired with back problems after winning the first set of the dead rubber against Chiudinelli only added to the sense that the fourth rubber was the decisive one. The Swiss may yet look back on their weekend in Fribourg as a very good investment in a team that now doesn't have to depend on one man, even if that man is the undisputed best in the world. ●

FRANCE v SWEDEN

DESPITE BEING A MONTH later than normal, the five Europe-based first-round ties took place amid a bleak mid-winter's snow. The late winter struck with a vengeance as February turned to March, and one of the coldest places in western Europe was Strasbourg, the Alsatian capital that staged the finely balanced tie between France and Sweden.

There was so much uncertainty surrounding who would play for which team that it was perhaps no surprise that the hero proved to be the one man who knew he was playing, and was confident in his ability to do the job his captain asked of him.

Paul-Henri Mathieu had a baptism of fire in Davis Cup by BNP Paribas. For much of 2003 and 2004 his name was synonymous with losing a two-sets-to-love lead in the fifth rubber of the 2002 Final. But if his impressive five-sets win over Carlos Moya in the 2004

Semifinal in Alicante brought confidence in his Davis Cup nerve flooding back, this tie sealed his rehabilitation, as the 23-year-old came through a nerve-wracking live fifth rubber to emerge as the latest product from Guy Forget's factory of players who punch above their weight when playing for their country.

Significantly, Mathieu had played on the Latin American clay court circuit while his two singles opponents, Joachim Johansson and Thomas Johansson (no relation), had gone from Australia to the European indoor events.

"It was certainly a plus for me," said Mathieu. "I felt very good on the court, and I was able to play two very good matches."

This contrasted with Joachim Johansson, Mathieu's first-day opponent, who had won the title in Adelaide in the first week of the year and then set a new record for aces in a match at the Australian Open by serving 51 against Andre Agassi (he still lost the match—remarkably in just four sets). Following his US Open semifinal six months earlier, he was the big new Swede, knocking on the door of the world's top ten.

By ranking, Mathieu should have been the underdog. He was conceding 88 places between his 99th and Johansson's 11th, but comfort on clay proved invaluable. With a strategy based around careful targeting of the Johansson backhand, Mathieu played a quality match, winning 6–3 6–4 6–2 in barely over two hours.

That should have broken Sweden's back, but France's captain, Guy Forget, had taken a gamble in recalling Sebastien Grosjean for his first Davis Cup tie since April 2003. Grosjean should have beaten Thomas Johansson on clay, the surface the Swede is least happy on, but Grosjean had missed most of the second half of 2004 with a nagging leg injury, and was badly short of match practice. The result was a surprisingly one-sided Swedish victory of 6–4 6–4 7–6(1).

That threw the advantage right back to Sweden, who, in the absence of Fabrice Santoro, were favorites for the doubles. The combination of the experienced Jonas Bjorkman with the in-form Simon Aspelin, a champion in Delray Beach and Memphis in the month preceding the tie, was expected to be too hot for Arnaud Clement and Michael Llodra to handle. But Clement, standing in for Santoro and supposedly the weak link in the French team, played the dominant role in a 7–6(5) 6–4 6–7(4) 6–4 win that reinstated the French as favorites.

Such was Clement's confidence after the doubles that there was a case for him to replace Grosjean against Joachim Johansson in the first reverse singles. Forget stuck with his original nomination, and probably wished he hadn't. Grosjean again displayed signs of rustiness, as Johansson won 3–6 6–1 6–4 6–1.

That set up a live fifth rubber, putting Mathieu back in that position for the first time since the 2002 Final. Some superb returning saw him open up a two-sets-to-love lead over Thomas Johansson, and he broke in the first game of the third set. At 5–4 with two hours 18 minutes played, Mathieu stood on the brink of putting France into the quarterfinals. But he missed a forehand on his first match point, and Johansson gave him no chance on the second. The set went into the tiebreak, and Johansson won it 7–4.

When the Swede broke to lead 3–1 in the fourth, the 6,000 spectators in the Rhenus Sport arena could have been forgiven for thinking back to the Final in Paris-Bercy in 2002. Would lightning strike twice? Mathieu was convinced it wouldn't.

Pictured from top:

Sebastien Grosjean (FRA) endured a frustrating weekend;

Joachim Johansson (SWE); Thomas Johansson (SWE)

Pictured over (from top left, clockwise):

Arnaud Clement and Michael Llodra have formed a formidable doubles pairing for the French; Paul-Henri Mathieu (FRA) was the fifth-rubber hero this time around; The French team show their gratitude to Mathieu

"I didn't have any match points against Youzhny," he said later. "It was a very different situation. The press have talked a lot about that defeat, but I had processed it several months later, certainly by the time I played Moya [September 2004], so I wasn't worried."

Johansson's comeback proved just a blip. He saved a third match point on his own serve at 4–5, but in the same game, Mathieu played another superb return on his fourth match point, followed it up with an unplayable forehand, and the victory was his. ●

RUSSIA v CHILE

2005 COULD HAVE BEEN Chile's year in the Davis Cup by BNP Paribas, but it was not to be.

Strange though it seems, the era when Chile produced a world No. 1 and Grand Slam finalist also witnessed the South American nation's dark age in the team competition. Marcelo Rios could never find enough back-up and never produced his best in Davis Cup for Chile to get into the elite 16-nation World Group. Other factors got in the way too, particularly in 2000 when Chile was due to play Morocco in the Play-offs, but were banned following the unruly behavior of their supporters at a home tie. But it wasn't until 2004 that a two-man Chilean team took representative tennis by storm.

With Chile in the Play-offs once again, Fernando Gonzalez and Nicolas Massu captured the tennis event at the Athens Olympics. The pair won the doubles gold medal in the small hours of the penultimate morning in Athens, Gonzalez having just won a marathon bronze medal play-off match against Taylor Dent. And then defying tiredness, Massu came back to beat Mardy Fish in a four-hour gold medal singles match. Two golds for Massu, a gold and a bronze for Gonzalez, and a few weeks later Chile back in the World Group for the first time since 1985. Confidence was so high that even an away draw against the mercurial Russians didn't seem unwinnable.

But then, in the second round of the 2005 Australian Open, Massu felt pain in a toe on his right foot. He retired after eight games against Philipp Kohlschreiber and found he had a stress fracture, which would take several weeks to heal. He was out of the visit to Moscow, and—with the greatest respect to Adrian Garcia—Chile was back to being pretty much a one-man team. With Garcia, the 117th-ranked Chilean No. 3, suddenly promoted to playing singles against the newly crowned Australian Open champion Marat Safin on a fast Taraflex court he had never played on, Chile's chances rested with Gonzalez.

Yet by the time Safin and Garcia took to the court, Chile was 1–0 up, Gonzalez having used his big-hitting game to great effect in defeating Russia's hero from the 2002 Final, Mikhail Youzhny 7–6(4) 5–7 6–3 7–6(4). The fast carpet came to Gonzalez's aid, his big serve registering 23 aces as the 19th-ranked player gave his team a chance. And his win seemed to have done major damage, as Youzhny confessed to having played so badly he felt Russia's best chance was to win 3–1 and avoid the need for a fifth rubber in which he would feature.

For that to happen, Marat Safin needed to play a significant role, yet his form since winning his second Grand Slam title five weeks earlier had not been impressive. Perhaps

Pictured from top:
Adrian Garcia (CHI); Mikhail Youzhny (RUS)
Pictured opposite:
Fernando Gonzalez (CHI) is always
passionate about representing his country

Pictured from top:
Marat Safin and Mikhail Youzhny (RUS); Marat Safin (RUS)

RUSSIA v CHILE CONTINUED

fortunate to be playing a lowly ranked opponent, Safin labored to a 6–1 3–6 6–3 7–6(4) win despite 62 unforced errors, finishing the match on his 15th ace.

With the scores tied at 1–1 and Garcia having gained some confidence from his match with Safin, Russia's captain Shamil Tarpischev was likely to change his nominated doubles team of Igor Andreev and Nikolay Davydenko. Safin and Youzhny had played together twice before and won both times, so they were called into action against Gonzalez and Garcia. Had it been Gonzalez and Massu, Chile would have been favorites. Even with Gonzalez and Garcia the Russians were only marginally better on paper, but in practice it proved one-way traffic, Safin and Youzhny winning 6–3 6–4 6–3 in an hour and a half.

"Marat served unbelievably today," said Gonzalez after the match, a reflection also that the Chileans had served particularly badly.

Gonzalez also knew that the destiny of the tie was now out of his hands. Even if he were to beat Safin, the chances of Garcia winning a live fifth rubber against Youzhny, Davydenko, or Andreev were slim, but he still pulled out everything for the rubber of the tie, a five-set classic against Safin which saw three tiebreaks and a gutsy fight back by the Chilean.

The first two tiebreaks went to Safin, but without any breaks of serve. Gonzalez then broke twice to take the third set, and another break-free fourth set was decided on a tiebreak, this time in Chile's favor. But then midway through the final set, Gonzalez played one bad game, was broken, and Safin served out the victory.

"The way we lost is a real shame," said a demoralized Gonzalez, who broke Safin twice but paid a bigger price for his one dropped serve. "We played five sets, and a few points changed the history of the match."

And perhaps the Davis Cup for 2005. Safin admitted to playing badly, adding: "We were lucky Massu didn't come. If he had played, I'm not sure how it would have all turned out."

But champions need luck. When the French general Napoleon Bonaparte interviewed potential officers, he is supposed to have asked them: "Are you lucky?" The champion nation of 2002 was through to meet the French team it had beaten in that Final—but had it used up its ration of luck for 2005? ●

ARGENTINA v CZECH REPUBLIC

A LOOK AT THE scores in the Argentina v Czech Republic tie gives the impression that this was a somewhat dull one-sided tie. But while the tie was indeed one-sided, the home side sealing victory by Saturday night via three four-set wins, this was perhaps the most colorful and emotional of the eight first round encounters.

The experience that everyone at the Buenos Aires Lawn Tennis Club will never forget came in the hour after Argentina had secured its place in the quarterfinals by winning the doubles. In the crowd were some 30 youngsters with learning disabilities, participants in a Special Olympics program in Argentina. They had been offered tickets for the doubles and told to be ready to hit some balls after the match had finished, but none of them could have expected the exhilarating experience they and the 6,000-strong crowd were to enjoy.

With David Nalbandian and Guillermo Canas still warming down after their victory, and Guillermo Coria trying to get his voice back after screaming his lungs dry from the Argentinean bench, the 30 youngsters were brought down to the main court of the August Club, the nerve center of Argentinean tennis that dates from 1892. Spontaneously, the players got out their rackets and began hitting with the youngsters. The impromptu hit became the centerpiece of a giant party, with experienced tennis watchers finding tears of joy streaming down their faces as the kids hit with and ultimately embraced their tennis-playing idols in the experience of a lifetime.

The impromptu party wrapped up 20 ecstatic days for Argentinean tennis. On February 15 the country's new Davis Cup captain, Alberto Mancini, had named his team. Mancini had taken over from Gustavo Luza, who, though highly respected in tennis circles, was not quite at one with his players even before the 2004 Quarterfinal defeat to Belarus. After that 5–0 drubbing, Luza resigned, and all of Argentina's top players voted on who they wanted to replace him. Mancini knew he had a mandate.

The team he announced on February 15 was the strongest-ever in Argentina's history—four players in the top 11! Remarkably, Coria and Nalbandian were playing for only the second time together in a Davis Cup by BNP Paribas tie, and the first at home.

The tie caught the imagination of the Buenos Aires public. Tennis had been one of Argentina's success stories during a perilous period in the country's economic history, but there were few chances to see the great generation of players on home soil. Here at the epicenter of Argentinean tennis would be the top four, and Davis Cup fever gripped the newspapers, television stations, and shop windows in the days leading up to the tie. Even Gaston Gaudio's withdrawal with a leg injury, which led to his replacement by Agustin Calleri, did nothing to dampen the enthusiasm.

In the first rubber, Nalbandian obviously felt the weight of expectation from the home fans, who were hoping for an easy victory against a Czech side no longer able to rely on Jiri Novak for all three days, and the Argentine got off to a slow start. Whether the watering of the court after Novak had won the first set influenced the result is hard to say, but from the start of the second set Nalbandian started to find his range in his first clay court match since Roland Garros nine months earlier. He broke the tiring Novak five times to take the match 4–6 6–2 6–3 6–4.

Tomas Berdych came to Buenos Aires as one of only three men to have beaten Roger Federer in the previous nine months. But he was struggling in the year after his breakthrough year, and he had only a good second set to show for his efforts against Coria, who was still not match-tight after a three-month layoff following shoulder surgery in August 2004. Coria's 6–3 3–6 6–0 6–3 win had flashes of brilliance, but a more confident opponent might have made more of the Argentinean's lack of form.

The Czech captain, Cyril Suk, said before the tie that the balance of power was stacked 99–1 in Argentina's favor, and that proved accurate in another one-sided match on Saturday. Suk resisted the temptation to call on the experienced Novak, trusting the relatively scratch pairing of Jan Hernych and Tomas Zib against the experienced Nalbandian

Pictured from top:

David Nalbandian (ARG); Tomas Berdych (CZE)

ARGENTINA v CZECH REPUBLIC CONTINUED

and Canas. Nalbandian, so underestimated as a doubles player in an era when the top singles stars infrequently play doubles on the tour, was the outstanding member of the quartet, as Argentina sealed its fourth quarterfinal in as many years with a 6–3 4–6 6–1 6–2 victory that unleashed the party.

The Czech players had a few concerns about the exuberance of the home support, and on the occasions when members of a soccer-like crowd called out at inappropriate moments they may well have had a point. But they were also wise enough to recognize that even the most impeccably behaved Buenos Aires crowd would not have helped them. Instead, the Czechs' most colorful contribution to the one-sided weekend was a breathtaking pyramid dance performed by the players at the official dinner, which ensured that they left having created a good impression.

Two wins on Sunday made the score 5–0, and perhaps that was inevitable given the two line-ups and Argentina's home advantage. But the sense in Buenos Aires was that more than just a comfortable first round victory had been achieved. It was a feeling that something had begun, that the country's immense talent had finally been channelled into a team in which all parties were working together. The quarterfinals were to provide the test of that team: away from home on the Argentineans' least-favorite surface. ●

AUSTRALIA v AUSTRIA

WHEN THE DRAW FOR the 2005 World Group was made, Austria had just had three players in the third round of the US Open for the first time. Stefan Koubek, Jürgen Melzer, and Alexander Peya had all hit form together, and with Julian Knowle enhancing his reputation on the doubles circuit, Austria suddenly had its strongest team since Thomas Muster, Horst Skoff, and Alex Antonitsch took the Alpine country to the 1990 semifinals.

The draw sent them to Australia's portable grass court, installed for the first time in the Olympic tennis arena in Sydney, but even away from home, the Austrians still posed a tricky assignment for an Australian team heavily dependent on the world No. 2 Lleyton Hewitt.

But Koubek was serving a suspension for a failed drug test, so Austria's most experienced player was out of the frame. Melzer, a former Wimbledon junior champion, still had pedigree to bring to the tie, and Austria's doubles team was always going to be a match for the aging Todd Woodbridge and Wayne Arthurs. But Koubek's absence somehow upset the fine balance, and the weekend proved relatively straightforward for the 28-time Davis Cup champions.

In fact, there seemed to be greater interest in the four-carat diamond engagement ring—reported to be worth 250,000 Australian dollars—that Hewitt had presented his fiancée, Bec Cartwright, a few weeks earlier. Having broken up with Kim Clijsters late in 2004, Hewitt had been with Cartwright constantly during the 2005 Australian Open, and they had announced their engagement the day after Hewitt lost the Melbourne final to Marat Safin. But by then many Australian tennis journalists had left town, so the Davis Cup in Sydney, the city in which Hewitt and Cartwright had just bought a new house, gave the media access to the newest romance in tennis.

Pictured opposite from top:
The impromptu hit between the Argentine team and local youngsters was a highlight of the tie; The Argentine team is a close-knit unit

Pictured from top:
Guillermo Coria (ARG); Jiri Novak (CZE)

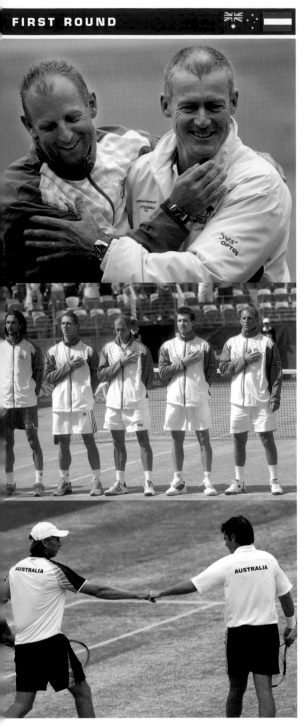

Hewitt admitted to knowing little about Alexander Peya before the two opened the tie, and by the end of a 6–2 6–3 6–4 win, he knew that the Austrian had a good game but not one to trouble the former world No. 1.

That might have played into Austria's hands for the second reverse singles, in which Melzer needed to beat Wayne Arthurs. The 33-year-old Australian came to Sydney straight from his first title on the main tour, having won in Scottsdale five days earlier, just two weeks after a run in Memphis that had seen him beat Melzer. But his Scottsdale triumph meant he arrived jetlagged in Sydney on the Tuesday, and took to the court against Melzer having practiced for just two hours.

The conditions were therefore ripe for Melzer to level the score, but Arthurs delivered what he described as one of the best matches of his career, inflicting a 7–6(5) 6–2 6–4 defeat of his fellow left-hander in just over two hours.

"I'd put it probably in my top three, along with obviously the Kafelnikov match [Davis Cup, Brisbane, 1999 when Arthurs won in four sets] and maybe a couple of my doubles matches along the way," he said.

Things might have been very different had Melzer won the first-set tiebreak. He led 5–3, but a call then went against him, and Arthurs reeled off four points to take the tiebreak 7–5. After that the Australian's confidence rocketed, and the Austrians were left feeling it just wasn't going to be their weekend.

That feeling grew on the Saturday, when rain came to the rescue of the Australians after the visitors had put themselves in a useful position. With Woodbridge getting frustrated with the way his serves were sitting up on what should have been a fast court, he lost four of his first six service games as the Austrian team of Knowle and Melzer took the first set. Though Knowle was broken in the second to allow the home side to level, Woodbridge's problems continued, Arthurs began feeling the air miles in his legs, and Austria were cruising. But then at 4–1 in the third set, the heavens opened.

That allowed Arthurs to have a massage, and Woodbridge to talk to Australia's coach, Wally Masur. Afterward Woodbridge said: "I was playing on a grass court but hitting my serves as if I was on clay. I was doubting myself the first couple of sets, and didn't play positively. Wally told me to try and play the way I play my best, and that was to be creative. I came back out and used my feet better and I played some nice lob volleys and was more aggressive. I had the attitude that if I was going to lose, to lose it swinging. The rain was crucial for me."

Though Woodbridge was broken on the resumption, the Australians were fresher. They broke Knowle in the third game of the fourth set, which sufficed to take the match into a decider. That went with serve, but in the 11th game, Melzer double-faulted on break point, and Woodbridge served out the 4–6 6–3 2–6 6–4 7–5 victory to love.

The second-most successful nation in the Davis Cup's history went through to the quarterfinals 5–0 after wins in the dead rubbers, and with Argentina known to be the next opponents, Australia decided to leave the portable grass court in place for four months, so it would seem less portable and—hopefully for the Aussies—play more like a permanent grass court when the clay-loving Argentineans came to town in July. ●

Pictured from top:
Captains Thomas Muster (AUT), left, and John Fitzgerald (AUS);
The Austrian team; Wayne Arthurs and Todd Woodbridge have
been stalwarts in doubles for the Australians
Pictured opposite:
Lleyton Hewitt (AUS) was as usual focused on the task for his country

BETTER ON THE BENCH?

The pressure of playing for one's country is one of the most intriguing aspects of Davis Cup, but it can be just as intense for those other members of the team—and the captain—watching from the sidelines.

Name
IVAN LJUBICIC

Born
MARCH 19, 1979,
IN BANJA LUKA,
BOSNIA & HERZEGOVINA

Turned professional
1998

Ivan Ljubicic won the "player of the round" poll on www.daviscup.com, claiming a convincing 61% of votes cast for his performance for Croatia against USA in Carson. He defeated Andre Agassi, Andy Roddick, and—in the doubles alongside Mario Ancic—the Bryan brothers in one amazing weekend.

PLAYER OF THE ROUND

ONE OF THE ABIDING images of the 2005 Davis Cup by BNP Paribas was the calm skyward glance that Ivan Ljubicic delivered when he aced Andy Roddick to see Croatia into the quarterfinals. No fist-pumping, no hysterical saluting—but then that would have been out of character for a man whose life experiences have taught him exactly where to place the significance of a tennis match.

Ljubicic was 12 when civil war struck his homeland. He hails from Banja Luka in Bosnia, one of the place names that became synonymous with the atrocities, violence, and human suffering that followed the breakup of Yugoslavia in the early 1990s. Young Ivan even came face to face with war when his father, Marko, frustrated at what a two-month military curfew was doing to his restless son, tried to get him to a tennis court. "We got as far as the control point," Ljubicic recalled in an interview with Deuce magazine, "and they were pointing guns at us and asking where we were going. It was not pleasant, in fact, we realized it was becoming impossible."

Marko arranged for Ivan to move to Italy, where a club was offering a few places to promising players from war-torn areas to further their tennis education. That was the break Ljubicic needed, but once on the full tour, his rise up the rankings was relatively slow.

The big breakthrough came in the small hours of an August 2004 morning in Athens. Ljubicic and his Croatian teammate Mario Ancic had been beaten in the semifinals of the Olympic tournament and were playing off for the bronze medal against Leander Paes and Mahesh Bhupathi. At 1:05 a.m., Ljubicic and Ancic won 7–6(5) 4–6 16–14 and went into near-ecstatic celebrations with the 1,500 or so mainly Croatian spectators who had stayed behind in anticipation of their triumph. It was an image to knock on the head any lingering notion that an Olympic medal is not valued by tennis players.

That injected the necessary confidence into Ljubicic that allowed him to tee off 2005 so impressively, both on the tour and in Davis Cup. Yet the leading tennis representative of a sports-mad and fiercely patriotic nation has remained quietly levelheaded about his success.

"People are patriotic in Croatia," he says. "We are a small country. Every success of a national team is really nice for them. There were a lot of good articles after the Davis Cup win against America. I was pleased with the way it was presented; it was really nice. But for me I didn't feel it that way. For me it was a very personal feeling, because obviously beating Andre is a great achievement—even though he is 35, he is one of the greats, and to beat him in the States is great—and against Andy I had a really bad record and I wanted to improve that, and that match was the key to the whole tie."

Having married his longtime girlfriend, Aida, in November 2004, Ljubicic gives the impression of contentment on and off the court. He looks like he will one day make a good father, and might even have grandchildren to bore with his exploits on the tennis tour in the 2000s. So what will he be telling them? "It's difficult for me to pick between winning the bronze medal at the Olympic Games and the Davis Cup. The Olympics and beating America happened within six months of each other, but I hope there's more I'll be able to talk to them about. But you know, for me personally nothing really changed. Why should I look at myself differently? Obviously it was proof that I can do important things, but I knew I could do it and hope I can do more before I finish playing."

Make that a very good father. ●

quarterfinals 15–17 JULY

Slovak Republic defeated Netherlands 4–1   BRATISLAVA, SLOVAK REPUBLIC—INDOOR HARD

Argentina defeated Australia 4–1   SYDNEY, AUSTRALIA—OUTDOOR GRASS

Russia defeated France 3–2   MOSCOW, RUSSIA—INDOOR CLAY

Croatia defeated Romania 4–1   SPLIT, CROATIA—INDOOR CARPET

Pictured on previous page:

Mario Ancic (left) and Ivan Ljubicic sent Croatia

into the semifinals for the first time

Pictured from top:

Could French Captain Guy Forget work his magic again?

The Argentine team arrived in Sydney as underdogs...

..against a confident Australian side very much at home on grass.

QUARTERFINALS

THE SHOCKS OF THE first round—in particular the demise of Spain and the USA—had left the 2005 Davis Cup by BNP Paribas looking to be very much the domain of central and eastern Europe. No one should have been too surprised at this.

A look through the draws of the Grand Slam junior tournaments in the first five years of the 21st century testified to the growing influence of players from eastern Europe, many of them keen to use success in tennis as a vehicle toward financial freedom and a passport to see the world. While the big names at the start of 2005 still came largely from America, Australia, and the countries of western Europe, it was only a matter of time before the emerging countries from the former eastern bloc would make their presence felt at the highest level.

Yet in a quarterfinal lineup that seemed to provide two bumper ties and two offering chances for lesser-fancied nations, the most obvious outcome seemed to be progress toward a final involving the two surviving Grand Slam nations, France and Australia. After all, the Australia tie was at home to a clay-court nation, Argentina, on grass, while France was up against a weakened Russian team in a tie made for the influential French captain Guy Forget to work his magic.

How wrong that scenario would prove. ●

AUSTRALIA v ARGENTINA

AUSTRALIA AT HOME ON grass in the Davis Cup! For years that combination seemed a guarantee of success. Even without the strength in depth that Harry Hopman and Neale Fraser had at their disposal when they captained Australia from 1949 to 1993 for an aggregate of 44 years, Australia still boasted the world No. 2 and Wimbledon semifinalist Lleyton Hewitt, and the grass-court specialist Wayne Arthurs, for the visit of Argentina, a nation laden with talent but still seemingly as frightened of grass as a dandelion in the path of a lawnmower.

Yet this was a watershed tie in several respects. It showed Australia's overdependence on Hewitt, especially after the record-breaking doubles specialist Todd Woodbridge had announced his retirement two weeks earlier at Wimbledon. It also showed that Australia's portable grass court was not the asset it was intended to be—this was its fourth outing, and by the end of the weekend Australia's record on it of two wins and two defeats was hardly what the home team had hoped for.

The biggest watershed, however, came for Argentina. This was the team that had lost all but one of its World Group away ties in the previous 14 years, the only victory coming in February 2004 against a weakened Moroccan side whose most fit player was ranked 411. Argentina did not travel well. Members of the Argentinean entourage did not always seem to take as much pleasure in exploring foreign cities as others on the global tennis circuit often do, and though a colossus on the clay of Buenos Aires, Argentina was a byword for vulnerability away from home. All that changed over the three days of Sydney.

There was a feeling leading up to the tie that the Argentineans were not going to be the pushover that some Australians clearly expected. At Wimbledon, their players had

proved they could win matches on grass. David Nalbandian reached the quarterfinals, and Guillermo Coria showed some good grass-court skills in reaching the round of 16 before losing to the eventual runner-up, Andy Roddick. True, the withdrawal of Guillermo Canas following a positive doping test had robbed the visitors of their top-ranked player, but the optimism in the Argentinean camp was palpable.

Whether it was part of the visitors' plan for Coria to try and rile Hewitt in the opening singles might never be known. Both men have done their fair share of getting under opponents' skin, and with Hewitt having been involved in an edgy match with Argentina's Juan-Ignacio Chela at the Australian Open six months earlier, the potential was immense for the sparks to fly against Coria. Neither man covered himself in glory on a damp and drizzly opening day in Sydney, and both later claimed they were the innocent victims. To the Australians, Hewitt's behavior was no different from normal—he certainly felt he did nothing wrong and said Coria was just a "sore loser." To the Argentineans, even Hewitt's normal behavior can be irritating, and Coria merely reacted to Hewitt's provocation. Coria said later: "Off the court he is one thing, but on the court you really feel like killing him."

In terms of the tennis, it was Hewitt who did the killing, winning 7–6(5) 6–1 1–6 6–2. Coria missed his chance in the first set, having led 4–2 with four break points for 5–2. He came within two points of winning the set when Hewitt served at 3–5, but once Hewitt had held, broken back, and then taken the last two points of the tiebreak from 5–5, the wind went out of Coria's sails. A break in the third game of the third set allowed Coria to stage a revival, but once Hewitt had broken in the fifth game, that was it, and the more he orchestrated the crowd after his winners, the more Coria fumed as the spectacle seemed to overwhelm him.

And yet, and yet, and yet. How much did that piece of drama take out of Hewitt? It's easy to believe the South Australian is indefatigable, that he runs on batteries that never need recharging. But he is human, and he had had to work very hard for his Wimbledon comeback after breaking two ribs in a freak domestic accident in May, so his reserve tank was a little less full than normal. Also, for all his fierce competitiveness on court, he is a man with standards and principles off court, and despite his protestations about doing nothing wrong against Coria, there was probably a part of him that was mildly unsettled. For whatever reason, he wasn't the same for the rest of the weekend. And he was about to meet his match in the form of David Nalbandian.

Nalbandian's run to the 2002 Wimbledon final, where he lost to Hewitt, inevitably meant he was going to carry most of Argentina's hopes in Sydney. He would probably have liked to play first, and taking the court against the dangerous Wayne Arthurs after Hewitt's win added further pressure. But the man from Cordoba knew his responsibility and was determined to do justice to it. It was to be one of the defining weekends of his career.

His 6–3 7–6(8) 5–7 6–2 win over Arthurs was more emphatic than the score suggests. Nalbandian broke in the opening game and saved two set points in the second-set tiebreak as the match reached the zenith of its quality. A second rain delay of the day meant play resumed under lights, and when Nalbandian had three break points at 5–5 in the third, the match seemed minutes from ending. But Arthurs saved all three and

Pictured from top:

The portable grass court that Australia kept in place after the first round tie against Austria, with the heat lamps used to keep it healthy visible in the background; Lleyton Hewitt (AUS); Guillermo Coria (ARG)

51

promptly broke Nalbandian to take the third set. At that stage the match was suspended for the night, but Nalbandian was much the stronger on the resumption, breaking twice to wrap up victory on Saturday morning.

Despite Canas being Argentina's top-ranked singles player, his loss seemed likely to affect Argentina most in the doubles, where he had successfully teamed with Nalbandian against the Czech Republic in the first round. With Nalbandian clearly Argentina's top option in doubles, Alberto Mancini gambled with the shock Roland Garros finalist Mariano Puerta, who had bounced back admirably from a drugs-related suspension in late 2003/early 2004. But following his survival performance on clay, he had failed to register any form on grass, so it was an act of faith to throw him into the doubles, even with such an accomplished partner as Nalbandian.

Mancini's gamble worked. With both pairs playing together for the first time (Australia fielded Hewitt and Arthurs), Australia got off to the better start, opening up a 4–2 lead. But Hewitt was broken in the seventh game, the Aussies squandered a 5–3 lead in the tiebreak, and two more errors from Hewitt meant Argentina took the breaker 8–6. Having been a shade lucky in the first set, Argentina's confidence rose. And when Hewitt served to stay in the second set at 4–5, both Puerta and Nalbandian pounced on his serves to break for 2–0. From that point the Argentineans were an exemplary combination—they broke Arthurs to lead 5–3 in the third, and with Nalbandian on fire, there was no way back for the hosts, Argentina winning 7–6(6) 6–4 6–3.

"It's amazing," said Nalbandian, "two points in one day. It's perfect for the team. I played very good in the last set of the singles and then with Mariano in the doubles we played almost perfect."

From the vantage point of Saturday night it was quite plausible to imagine Hewitt could bounce back and beat Nalbandian, but with the benefit of hindsight, the die was cast. If not broken, Hewitt's spirit had taken a battering. Nalbandian was in the ascendant, and he was never going to lose the first reverse singles. In fact it took him just an hour and 54 minutes to win 6–2 6–4 6–4 to post his first win over the Australian in four matches. He even had the confidence to change his game plan early in the first set: "I saw Lleyton was so nervous in the beginning," he said, "that I changed a little bit in my mind the way to play him. I knew that if it came to long rallies, he was going to miss before I would."

Speaking a few weeks later, Nalbandian said: "I think I played an incredible weekend, and it took me a while to come down from it. I took four days off before starting to practice for the hard courts. I learned a lot in Sydney: I gained confidence; I learned that I can be a tough opponent for anyone, even away from home; I think it will make me mentally strong on a permanent basis; but most of all I learned that I really love Davis Cup. It's an incredible feeling inside all the players, playing for their country. It's not the same as playing on the tour. I feel the whole country behind us, cheering for us. I felt very proud to be part of the team. It was particularly important for Argentina to do well after we were unlucky to lose an important player." ●

Pictured from top:

Lleyton Hewitt (left) and Wayne Arthurs (AUS); Wayne Arthurs (AUS); David Nalbandian was in inspired form for Argentina over the weekend

Pictured opposite:

David Nalbandian (ARG); The Argentine team celebrates a famous victory

SLOVAK REPUBLIC
v NETHERLANDS

SOMEONE OUGHT ONE DAY to write a manual about how to approach hopeless causes in the Davis Cup by BNP Paribas. If anyone ever does, it should take a good look at the Netherlands' attitude to the Quarterfinal in the Slovak National Tennis Center in Bratislava.

The Dutch just squeezed through their first round tie against a Swiss team lacking Roger Federer. For that they at least had Sjeng Schalken. For the Quarterfinal against the Slovak Republic, both Schalken and Martin Verkerk were absent, and the only Top-100 player available to the Dutch captain, Tjerk Bogtstra, was Peter Wessels at 89. Bogtstra originally nominated Wessels, the experienced through frustratingly erratic Raemon Sluiter, Rogier Wassen, and Dennis van Scheppingen. He then shocked most observers by dropping Wassen and van Scheppingen in favor of a 26-year-old Davis Cup debutant, Melle van Gemerden, and a player he plucked from the Wimbledon over-35s invitation tournament, Paul Haarhuis. Perhaps inevitably, the Slovak Republic won, but not by much and with the Dutch ruing two significant injuries over the weekend.

The Dutch under Bogtstra have punched above their weight. The 38-year-old coach was brought in as a stopgap in 2001 when the Dutch players wanted Haarhuis to become captain but Haarhuis declined to take on the role while still a player. Since Bogtstra took over, his quiet but assured manner has commanded great respect from his players, and his record with virtually no Top-Ten players includes the Netherlands' only semifinal showing (in 2001). Little wonder he maintained the captaincy when Haarhuis retired from playing in early 2004.

But Bogtstra knows when age is no barrier to class, and amid the carnage of his injury list, he noted that Haarhuis and Ellis Ferreira had won the Wimbledon over-35s. Why not bring back the wily 39-year-old for another Davis Cup doubles? Asked at the post-draw press conference whether he was still in adequate shape to play, Haarhuis replied: "No, but that's OK—I have nothing to do at home." It was wonderful psychology for a team facing near certain defeat!

In the end the doubles proved crucial, and while the record shows Karol Beck and Michal Mertinak having beaten Haarhuis and van Gemerden in four sets, it was genuinely close. Beck had looked weary and deflated at the end of his five-sets defeat to Wessels on the opening day, and had the doubles gone to a fifth set, he may have felt it again. Wessels himself suffered the recurrence of an injury he thought he was getting over. And who knows what might have happened had Sluiter not gotten a cramp after taking eight of nine games to set up a potentially winning position against Dominik Hrbaty in the opening singles?

But, luck or not, and with all respect to the way the Dutch made a fist of a seemingly hopeless cause, this was the Slovaks' moment. The hosts were clearly the better team, they demonstrated superb esprit de corps, and they deserved their moment of glory, for this was the first time the 12-year-old nation had made it to the Semifinals of the Davis Cup.

After beating Wessels to seal victory in the first reverse singles, Hrbaty said it was one of the best sporting moments in the Slovak Republic's history. "After ice hockey, where the Slovak Republic won the gold medal at the world championships, this is the second-biggest result for our country," he said. "As far as publicity is concerned, this is a great advantage for the Slovak Republic because ice hockey is only played in a few countries but tennis is played all over the world, so everyone will know about this."

After leading his nation to victory over Spain, Hrbaty was again the mainstay of the Slovak quarterfinal triumph. In the opening singles, he gained a 6–1 5–2 lead, only to see the

Pictured from top:
Dutch Captain Tjerk Bogtstra has instilled a real team spirit in the Netherlands' camp; Tjerk Bogtstra (Captain, NED)

two-handed Sluiter—who had never lost to Hrbaty in three previous meetings—bounce back with seven games to lead 2–0 in the third. The Dutchman was reveling on the quick indoor hard court, but at 3–1 he felt a click in his wrist, and while there was no major damage, the effort to make up the second-set deficit finally caught up with him. He suffered from a cramp in his right wrist, and shortly after, a cramp in his legs. From that healthy position he won just four more games, Hrbaty turning the screw to win 6–1 5–7 6–4 6–3 and dedicating the victory to his grandmother, who that day was celebrating her 80th birthday.

Wessels had made an impressive Davis Cup by BNP Paribas debut in March against the Swiss but was fighting off a rib injury in his singles against Beck. He had slipped on a clay court two weeks earlier and had bruised the rib, and in the course of the match against Beck, a passing shot struck the bruised spot. Though Wessels posted one of the best results of his career, winning 6–7(5) 7–5 6–7(3) 6–4 6–2 in four and a half hours after trailing 6–7 2–5, he was very stiff afterward and had to pull out of the doubles in which he was due to partner Haarhuis. Van Gemerden took his place.

Not that that seemed to weaken the Dutch pair, who took the first set against Mertinak and a revitalized Beck, whose sheer presence on the court was a testimony to his fitness and the fingers of the Slovak Republic's masseurs. It was a must-win match for the Dutch, as even in the absence of public knowledge about Wessels's injury, Hrbaty was strongly favored to win the first reverse singles. But gradually the Slovak pair got into the match. Inspired by some great lobbing by Beck, the Slovaks took the second and third sets, but the Dutch took an early break in the fourth. Beck and Mertinak broke back, but Haarhuis said afterward: "I never felt we would lose the match, even when we were two sets to one down." Yet in the 11th game van Gemerden's serve was broken, Beck finished the job with an unreturnable serve, and the biggest point of the weekend had gone to the hosts 5–7 6–3 6–4 7–5.

With Beck doubtful for the fifth singles, Hrbaty had to win, but this was his hour. Unfortunately, when the moment of triumph arrived, it was a little anticlimactic. For the first six games everything was level, but once Hrbaty broke in the seventh, Wessels's level slumped, and he won just one more game before retiring with his rib injury at 6–3 6–1 3–0 to unleash wild celebrations in the Sibamac Arena. The Slovak Republic's canny captain, Miloslav Mecir, recognized that injuries had played a part in his country's win, but this was the Slovak Republic's moment—and another important milestone in nation-building for the new states of central and eastern Europe. ●

CROATIA v ROMANIA

CROATIA IS ONLY A year and a half older than the Slovak Republic, having also emerged from the post-Soviet turmoil of the early 1990s. And like the Slovaks, the Croats reached their first-ever Davis Cup Semifinal in 2005. But the historical background was much more potent, and as a result, the euphoria in Split as Croatia beat Romania was that little bit more piquant.

When Czechoslovakia split into two separate countries in January 1993, it happened peacefully and by agreement. The same cannot be said of Croatia's birth. That came about

Pictured from top:
Raemon Sluiter (NED); Karol Beck (SVK);
The Slovak team celebrates victory

55

CROATIA v ROMANIA CONTINUED

during the bloody conflict within Yugoslavia, as Croatia—one of six states that made up Yugoslavia from 1918 to 1991—attempted to follow Slovenia's declaration of independence but got embroiled in a civil war with the Serb-led forces of the disintegrating country.

As the war reached its height, two Croats, Goran Ivanisevic and Goran Prpic, steered Yugoslavia's tennis team to the Davis Cup Semifinals in March 1991. It would have been Ivanisevic's third semifinal, but by September 1991 the two Gorans declined to play under the Yugoslav flag. There was an attempt to have the fledgling state of Croatia take Yugoslavia's place in the semifinals because the Yugoslav team had been exclusively Croatian, but its tennis association had not yet been recognized as a national association, so the ITF had little choice but to stick with Yugoslavia. That September, a weakened Yugoslav team lost heavily to the French.

By 1993 Croatia had entered the Davis Cup, and as a special dispensation to the two Gorans' achievements in 1991, the new nation was allowed into Europe/Africa Zone Group I rather than having to work its way up from the bottom. With Ivanisevic firmly established in the world's Top Ten, the sports-mad nation looked for golden days under its own distinctive checkered flag. Yet injury curtailed Prpic's career, Ivanisevic struggled for support, and the best Croatia could manage was one World Group appearance in 1995. Meanwhile Croatia's soccer players became the national sporting heroes, with their third place in the 1998 World Cup in France. Only during Ivanisevic's final days, in 2002 and 2003, did Croatia finally make it back to the World Group.

By then Croatia had the makings of a team. Ljubicic was firmly established in the Top 50, Ivo Karlovic was making progress up the rankings, and in Mario Ancic—a ballboy in Croatia's defeat to Australia in the 1996 Play-offs—the Croats had one of the most exciting teenagers in world tennis. And when Ljubicic and Ancic won the Olympic bronze medal in Athens, the foundations were laid for Croatia's best-ever Davis Cup year. The draw, pitting Croatia away to a powerful American team, seemed to have burst the bubble, but once Ljubicic had performed his heroics in Los Angeles, the road to the Final seemed kissed by Croatian sunshine, with the likelihood of three successive home ties to follow.

That's why, when Ljubicic took his Davis Cup record for 2005 to six wins out of six by beating Andrei Pavel to give Croatia a 3–1 lead, the celebrations in Ivanisevic's home town were on a par with those that followed his Wimbledon title in 2001—even though Ivanisevic himself was absent on the seniors tour. This young but intensely proud nation had achieved what it felt was its right 14 years earlier.

But for Croatia it wasn't plain sailing by the Adriatic Sea. Romania was never going to be an easy opponent in what was likely to be Andrei Pavel's last chance of Davis Cup glory. The 31-year-old had needed five opportunities to reach his first quarterfinal and wasn't going to let the prospect of Romania's first semifinal since the golden days of Ilie Nastase and Ion Tiriac in 1973 pass without a fight.

And on the first day Pavel shocked the hosts. Twice a set down, he came back to beat Ancic 1–6 6–4 4–6 6–3 6–4, the crucial moment having come in the second set when Ancic led 6–1 3–1 and had a break point to lead 4–1 with a double break. So often missed opportunities for a double break prove to be turning points, and that's what happened, as Ancic lost his way and Pavel notched up another impressive Davis Cup victory. Pavel put the

Pictured from top:
Croatia is a team in the true sense of the word; The Croatian team in jubilant mood; Croatian hero—again—Ivan Ljubicic
Pictured opposite:
Andrei Pavel struggled valiantly for Romania in his first Davis Cup by BNP Paribas Quarterfinal

CROATIA v ROMANIA CONTINUED

victory on a par with his win over Max Mirnyi in the first round, but knowing he would have to play on all three days, the three-hour-and-40-minute duration was an important factor.

At that stage, however, Romania seemed firmly in the driving seat. A margin of 1–0 may not be massive, but Ljubicic hadn't been playing as well in the second three months of the year as he played in the first three, and Victor Hanescu seemed to have a 50-50 chance going into the second singles. Ljubicic even admitted afterward that there was a lot more pressure on him than in the first round against the Americans. "I was aware that if we lost to Romania at home, everyone would have forgotten what happened in L.A. very, very quickly," he said. "So I felt the pressure much more in the quarterfinals. We were the favorites, and we were the ones who beat the Americans away, so everyone was looking at us already in the semifinals. And then Mario losing that first match didn't help at all."

As a result, Ljubicic's 6–3 6–2 7–6(3) win over Hanescu perhaps counts as being as great an achievement as beating Agassi and Roddick. Not only did he tap straight into his form from earlier in the year—"I started in fifth gear" was his description—but he never let the Romanian into the match. Even the third set was never really in doubt, Hanescu having to save break points in the ninth game and never being ahead in the tiebreak.

What would have happened if Romania had won the doubles will never be known. Certainly the visitors should have won it, and their pair of Pavel and Gabriel Trifu can be proud of the part they played in a four-hour classic.

Pavel and Trifu were twice a set up, the second time after a dramatic tiebreak in which they led 4–1, were pulled back to 4–4, had two set points at 6–4, saved a set point at 7–8, and finally converted their fifth set point on a Trifu service winner to take the breaker 11–9. When Ancic was broken at the start of the fourth set, Romania was on course for victory, but Croatia broke back, and then broke Trifu in the tenth game to level the match. Though the serving on the quick hard court remained excellent throughout the fifth set, in the tenth game Ancic and Ljubicic connected with some blistering returns, two serves Pavel felt were aces were called faults, and Croatia broke to take the crucial rubber 5–7 6–4 6–7(9) 6–4 6–4.

As everyone went to bed on Saturday night, the feeling was that the Croats had secured their place in the semifinals. Ljubicic was on a run of seven straight Davis Cup wins, and he would be opening up against Pavel, who had played ten sets in seven hours and 42 minutes. So when Ljubicic came out and beat the punch-drunk Romanian 6–3 6–4 6–3 to secure Croatia's first-ever Davis Cup by BNP Paribas Semifinal, it was little surprise. Pavel broke Ljubicic twice but didn't have the stamina to make his breaks count. "I sensed early that Pavel was slow," said Ljubicic, "and once I'd got back from 0–3 down in the second set, I knew I was going to win in three."

The heroics against Romania were less dramatic than those against America, but Ljubicic had once again seen his country home with three victories in three days. But it would be wrong to say he didn't make any mistakes. When packing his kit bag for the match against Pavel, he accidentally left a digital camera in it. Having won the match and seen the "soccer-like atmosphere" (Pavel's words) turn into a massive celebration with a somewhat premature rendering of the Queen hit "We are the champions," Ljubicic discovered his camera and took it out. "This will be a memory for the rest of my life," he said of the pictures taken at that moment of glory. ●

Pictured from top:

Mario Ancic (CRO); Victor Hanescu (ROM); Andrei Pavel (ROM)

Pictured opposite top to bottom:

Mario Ancic (left) and Ivan Ljubicic (CRO) brought Croatia the crucial doubles point against Gabriel Trifu (left) and Andrei Pavel (ROM)

RUSSIA v FRANCE

IF CROATIA AND ROMANIA were favorites to win their quarterfinals, the same could not have been said for the third eastern European team in the last four, Russia. All four ties were undecided going into the final day, but Russia's clash with France was the one that would produce the greatest upset, but perhaps the best spirit too.

Moscow's weather in July seemed to be a metaphor for the Russia-France Quarterfinal. It's largely hot, at times it can be scorching, but a brutal and violent thunderstorm is never far away, and when one comes, it can inflict severe damage for a good hour, after which the landscape somehow looks different.

Six weeks before Russia and France convened in Moscow, the outlook was sunny for the 2002 champions. Though he lost in five sets to Tommy Robredo in the round of 16, Marat Safin looked good on the clay of Roland Garros, and Nikolay Davydenko's run to the Paris semifinals meant Russia had two men in the world's Top Ten for the first time since Safin and Yevgeny Kafelnikov were at their peak.

Something else happened at Roland Garros that would influence the barometer of the quarterfinal. In the third round, France's Paul-Henri Mathieu played Guillermo Canas. The Frenchman came back from two sets down to set up four match points, but all four got away, a couple of them on hasty errors, and Canas won 8–6 in the fifth. Mathieu had done so much work to banish the idea that he was brittle on the big points, an unkind reputation dating back to the 2002 Davis Cup Final when he lost to Mikhail Youzhny from two sets up, yet here he was losing a match he should have won.

But after Paris a metaphorical thunderstorm hit the Russian camp. Safin announced he was suffering from an inflammation known as "jumper's knee" and would have to have treatment throughout July. Then at Wimbledon, Davydenko withdrew from his match against Jonas Bjorkman after taking the first set, complaining of an inflamed wrist. When he suffered the exact same fate in the first round in Gstaad two weeks later, Russia looked like it would have to face France without its top two singles players.

France was not at full strength either. Sebastien Grosjean, no longer the French No. 1 in ranking but still the first name Guy Forget would have penciled into his team notebook, said he needed time with his family. But with Forget able to bring in the 19-year-old Davis Cup debutant Richard Gasquet, it still seemed the French were slight favorites on a clay court laid not just for the Davis Cup Quarterfinal, but also for Russia's women's team, who had beaten USA the weekend before to reach the Fed Cup Final.

Russia's captain, Shamil Tarpischev, decided to gamble on Davydenko. With Youzhny still building up his fitness after a knee injury, the only fully fit player at Russia's disposal—other than Teimuraz Gabashvili, a youngster ranked outside the Top 200 brought in for the experience—was Igor Andreev. He was guaranteed a singles berth, at least on the opening day, and Davydenko's wrist seemed a better gamble than opting for Youzhny, given Davydenko's form (he had not only reached the semifinals in Paris but also the Australian Open quarterfinals).

When Andreev comes to tell his grandchildren about one of the best weekends of his career, he can be forgiven for leaving out the first two chapters of the story. In the first, he was blown away by Gasquet, who posted one of the best Davis Cup by BNP Paribas

Pictured from top:

Igor Andreev (RUS) looked out of sorts on day one and two; There was concern in the French camp on day one about Richard Gasquet's wrist; Despite his wrist problems, Gasquet made an impressive debut and won the opening rubber

debuts in recent years. But the victory came at a cost to France, one that only became apparent on the final day.

To say Gasquet was a prodigy would be an understatement. He was so gifted before his age was in double figures that he appeared on the cover of France's leading tennis magazine at nine, tagged as his country's great tennis hope. Though only five at the time, he claims to remember the ecstatic French Davis Cup triumph of 1991 in Lyon, and grew up with the dream of one day playing Davis Cup for France.

On July 15, 2005, that day came. Gasquet came to Russia as one of only three men to have beaten the world No. 1, Roger Federer, in the first six months of 2005. He had been so hyped up for the ten days leading up to his Davis Cup debut that he had hardly slept, and Forget's team had had to keep the lid on his excitement. When he finally stepped out on court, he played a superb match, beating Andreev 6–4 6–3 7–6(1). The first two sets were outstanding, Gasquet's variety and explosive forehands making Andreev look very ordinary and unimaginative.

But early in the third set Gasquet needed treatment. "I had stress cramps in my right wrist," he explained later. "I've been thinking of this match for the past ten days, I've been so keen to play, and I think this can happen. It's not the fatigue injury I had at Roland Garros, it's just a tension injury. But I'm so pleased to have won, I played nearly a perfect match."

Gasquet's wrist had survived, and Davydenko's did just as well in his 7–5 6–2 7–5 win over Mathieu. It might have been very different if Mathieu had converted one of the seven break points he had in the first set, certainly one of the two set points he had at 5–4. He came into the match having won his three previous Davis Cup rubbers against Carlos Moya, Joachim Johansson, and Thomas Johansson, but the psychological damage done by the Canas defeat weighed heavily in the first set, after which Davydenko was never again behind.

It was a match that fully justified the All Russian Tennis Association's decision to play indoors in Moscow's Olympic Stadium, as groundstrokes were pummeled to the sounds of rain pattering, lightning clattering, and thunder rumbling around the 25-year-old arena. While the sun shone for Davydenko for the first two and a half sets, the clouds gathered midway through the third. First he needed massage for tension cramps in his thighs, then he abandoned his conservative game plan at 5–2 and promptly found himself at 5–5. "My tactic was to play solidly from the baseline and make him make the mistakes," he explained. "The only time I didn't do that was in the third set, but I refound my plan in time to win in three."

Davis Cup by BNP Paribas is about teamwork, and France's teamwork was vastly superior in the doubles. In every respect their team of Arnaud Clement and Michael Llodra was better than Andreev and Youzhny, and only a poor couple of points midway through the third-set tiebreak prevented the French from winning in straight sets. Before the match Youzhny said he felt it would take a while for him and Andreev to gel in their first match together; Guy Forget said he had expected to see Andreev partnering Davydenko as the two play regularly on the tour; and Clement and Llodra were playing together for the 25th time in total and the third in Davis Cup.

When on the first point of the second game Andreev stayed back after his first serve and was jammed at his feet by a ferocious Clement return, the French could see their

Pictured from top:

Nikolay Davydenko was a solid performer all weekend for Russia;

Paul-Henri Mathieu (FRA) endured a disappointing tie;

The French doubles team of Michael Llodra (left) and Arnaud Clement were just too strong for Igor Andreev and Mikhail Youzhny (RUS)

BNP PARIBAS
BNP PARIBAS
BNP PARIBAS
BNP PARIBAS
RUSSIA
BOSS

RUSSIA v FRANCE CONTINUED

route to victory. They peppered Andreev, and despite Youzhny putting in a solid performance, the Russians could not prevent the French winning 7–5 6–4 6–7(3) 6–2.

So often the doubles decides the close Davis Cup ties, but not on this occasion. Davydenko came out on fire against Gasquet in the first reverse singles, and when the Frenchman trailed 6–2 2–0 the match looked won for the Russian. But little by little, Gasquet got himself back, and from 2–4 he reeled off four straight games to level at a set all.

That should have been the point for the match to become a contest, but suddenly the nervous energy Gasquet had expended against Andreev on Friday came back to haunt him. Davydenko broke in the first game of the third set, Gasquet suddenly felt exhausted, and Davydenko dropped just three games after that to win 6–2 4–6 6–2 6–1. Dodgy wrist or not, Davydenko had done his job for Russia.

As he signed well over a hundred autographs and embraced former Russian President Boris Yeltsin, everything seemed set for a repeat of the deciding match of the 2002 Final: Youzhny against Mathieu. Though Andreev was the nominated player, Youzhny had played much better in the doubles and had beaten Mathieu the three times they had played. But the change-of-player announcement never came, and so Andreev, who had won just one set in his two rubbers, took to the court against Mathieu. Once again the French seemed slight favorites.

This time the thunderstorm hit the French. Andreev played one of his better matches but must have thought his birthday had come early, so many gifts did he receive from his opponent. Anyone who has ever played tennis knows what it's like to have a day when simply nothing works. That was Mathieu's fate, but in the full glare of publicity.

For one and a half sets Andreev played beautiful tennis, going for the lines and hitting them with intense regularity. But even the six-game first set took 38 minutes, a sign that Mathieu was in the match, merely losing the crucial points. "I kept telling Paulo to hang in there," said Forget, "because we knew Andreev couldn't keep up that level forever."

Indeed he couldn't, but by the time the Russian's level dropped, Mathieu's confidence was so shot that he could do little to seize his opportunities. By the time he held serve for the first time he was a set and 4–1 down, frustratingly unimaginative and horrendously error-prone. There were plenty of chances for him, but the nightmare went on and on, and Andreev won 6–0 6–2 6–1 on an ace as the clock showed two hours one minute.

For the second time in four years Russia had come back from losing the doubles to beat the French on both final-day singles. It was a bitter blow for the traveling French fans—officially 118 of them, but they often made as much noise as a couple of thousand Russian supporters—but in a gesture that embodied the spirit of the competition, they chanted "Igor Igor" as Andreev left the court. Indeed the whole tie had been played in superb spirit, from the French banner on the opening day that read "I may be from France, but I still miss you Marat," to Mikhail Youzhny's dignified decision to enter the French locker room after the final rubber and say how close the tie had genuinely been and how lucky the Russians were to have won.

As the last supporters left the stadium, the sun was shining—certainly on Russia, but also on the Davis Cup. ●

Pictured from top:

Nikolay Davydenko kept his eye on the ball for Russia;
Igor Andreev came good on day three
Pictured opposite from top:
Doubles teams in action; Igor Andreev enjoyed the
traditional Davis Cup celebrations

CUP COLORS

Fans often take center stage on Davis Cup weekends, supporting their nations in the most colorful—and sometimes bizarre—ways.

Name
DAVID NALBANDIAN

Born
JANUARY 1, 1982,
IN CORDOBA,
ARGENTINA

Turned professional
2000

David Nalbandian won all three of the rubbers he played against Australia in the 2005 Quarterfinals, defeating Wayne Arthurs, Arthurs and Todd Woodbridge in the doubles alongside Mariano Puerta, and then Lleyton Hewitt to seal victory for Argentina—all on a grass court. No wonder users of www.daviscup.com voted him their player of the round for the quarterfinals, with 73% of votes cast.

PLAYER OF THE ROUND

THERE'S A MISCONCEPTION ABOUT Argentina in tennis circles. It is that the vast majority of the country's tennis courts are clay. That is largely true for the area around the capital, Buenos Aires, but travel northwest to Cordoba, and there are much greater numbers of hard courts.

One of them was built in the backyard of an Armenian immigrant by the name of Nalbandian, whose son, Norberto, had three sons: Javier, Dario, and David. From the age of five, David used to use the court to score points—psychological and tennis—against his elder brothers.

Eleven years later, he became the first Argentinean to win a junior Grand Slam singles title outside the clay of Paris. In the 1998 US Open final, he beat a promising Swiss boy, Roger Federer. The following year he looked set to add the Wimbledon title to his US title, only to turn up late for his semifinal against Jurgen Melzer and find he had been defaulted. Though he and his roommate, Guillermo Coria, went on to win the doubles, Nalbandian didn't return to Wimbledon until 2002. That meant that on the morning of his final against Lleyton Hewitt, he had yet to lose a singles match at Wimbledon—boys or main draw!

That record ended abruptly that afternoon, when Hewitt allowed him just six games in a very one-sided final. But Nalbandian had announced that he was a serious factor at the top of the game, and the following year he came within one point of reaching the US Open final, when he held match point against eventual champion Andy Roddick in the third set of their semifinal. After that, injuries blunted his progress, but as an all-around player who would have been very much at home in the era when the top singles players also played top-level doubles, Nalbandian will always have great opportunities in Davis Cup. The year 2005 proved to be his year, notably when he played the lead role in Argentina's unlikely but emphatic win against Australia on grass.

Nalbandian can remember watching Argentina's soccer team beat West Germany in the final of the 1986 World Cup, but it was watching Davis Cup that really inspired him. "I saw a lot of Davis Cup in Argentina, especially when we were in the World Group, and I was dreaming and saying one day I hope to be there. And now I am."

To many people associated with the global tennis circuit, Nalbandian is not the easiest guy around. Some of that is his inherent directness, and he was one of the loudest critics when he felt the promoter of the 2003 Tennis Masters Cup, the Texas furniture millionaire Jim McIngvale, was not showing as much respect to the six non-Americans in the field as he did to the two home players. Some of it may lie in the fact that many of the top Argentineans don't speak English in interviews, so Nalbandian perhaps gets saddled with more requests than he considers reasonable.

But then the feisty and determined qualities that enable a player to battle his way to the top of a highly competitive sport don't always make for charming and smooth-talking media personalities. Yet such people can be as interesting as they are difficult; and not every instance of irritation with public obligations is what it seems. After his win over Lleyton Hewitt that saw Argentina into the 2005 Semifinals, Nalbandian was giving a radio interview and was asked to sum up how the weekend left him feeling. "Amazing!" he replied and dashed off. To some it looked like impoliteness at a moment of triumph—in reality, he was just desperate to use the bathroom! ●

67

semifinals 23–25 SEPTEMBER

Slovak Republic defeated Argentina 4–1 BRATISLAVA, SLOVAK REPUBLIC—INDOOR HARD

Croatia defeated Russia 3–2 SPLIT, CROATIA—INDOOR CARPET

Pictured on previous page:
The Slovak team celebrated victory by shaving their heads
Pictured from top:
Victory meant so much to the Slovaks (top) and the Croatians

SEMIFINALS

LOOK AT ANY DRAW for a Grand Slam tournament, and it's fairly certain you'll find a shock result early on. And in most cases, you'll find that the lowly-ranked player who caused the shock will have lost in the next round. That's the problem—it's hard to follow up the high of a shock win with another win, especially if the second opponent is less illustrious than the first.

The same trap ought to apply to team tennis, but the 2005 Davis Cup Semifinal ties showed both the Slovak Republic and Croatia bucking the trend. Six months after they knocked out the 2004 finalists, Spain and the USA respectively, the two emerging nations were not only still in the draw, but managed to build on their unexpected success to reach their first-ever finals.

And where there is no history of success, the joy is so much more passionate.

SLOVAK REPUBLIC
v ARGENTINA

Hindsight is a great thing! The 4–1 score by which the Slovak Republic beat Argentina— and in particular the three live rubbers won by the Slovaks being in straight sets—makes it easy to forget just what strong favorites the Argentineans were coming into this Semifinal.

This was the team that had finally seemed to come together under Alberto Mancini's captaincy. The quietly spoken thirty-six-year-old, who, with Guillermo Vilas, Jose-Luis Clerc, and Martin Jaite belongs in a quartet of Argentina's most successful tennis players, seemed to have changed the culture in the Argentinean ranks. Not only did the South Americans pull off their great win in Sydney in the quarterfinals, but following that coup, Mancini had managed to persuade Gaston Gaudio to join the team. Just four months earlier at the World Team Cup, Gaudio and Guillermo Coria's relationship had become strained, with Gaudio suggesting he wouldn't play on the same team as Coria for the semifinals. But Mancini's quiet diplomacy had managed to smooth the ruffled feathers, and he was able to name a team consisting of the players placed eighth, ninth, tenth, and eleventh in the world rankings for the visit to Bratislava.

Not only that, but the week before the semifinals, Coria had reached the final in Beijing, losing to the world No. 2, Rafael Nadal, in a final set, and Coria and David Nalbandian had both reached the quarterfinals of the US Open two weeks earlier. With Nalbandian and Mariano Puerta presenting a formidable lineup in doubles, it was hard to see where the Slovak Republic could possibly pick up three points.

Dominik Hrbaty revealed how the home team felt it could win: "We need to beat Coria twice, and pick up one point from somewhere else."

It sounded easy, and the Slovaks did again have the advantage of their Premier hard court (which isn't a traditional hard court—it's a top layer of acrylic paint covering hard rubber about a millimeter deep, then four millimeters of soft rubber, and below that a concrete floor). But watching Coria and Nalbandian having long baseline rallies in practice, one found it hard to believe the court was really lightning fast. In fact the very first point of the weekend had sixteen strokes, so any suggestion that the surface was unfairly quick—and such suggestions were made in passing by the visitors during the practice days—can probably be dismissed as mind games in advance of the real thing. And whatever the speed of the surface, Argentina still seemed to hold most of the cards. A banner among the 150-or-so visiting supporters in the crowd read "You put the surface, we put the 'huevos'!" ("huevos" normally means "eggs" but here was used in its slang meaning of "gutsy fighters"), and that seemed to sum it up nicely.

So where did it all go wrong for the favorites? The most obvious explanation is also the simplest: they were beaten by a better team. Based on rankings, the Slovaks should have been underdogs in all five rubbers. But thanks to a well-honed team spirit nurtured by their captain, Miloslav Mecir, and the backing of four thousand vociferous supporters used to exercising their vocal chords at the neighboring Slovan Bratislava soccer and ice hockey stadiums and cheer-led by three drummers, they presented a brick wall the Argentineans were unable to break down.

There were various pivotal points in the weekend's action, but all of them went to the Slovak Republic. The first rubber between Coria and the 48th-ranked Karol Beck had a crucial period at the end of the first set, which went in Beck's favor. Had the Argentineans saved their fourth match point in the second tiebreak of the doubles and gone on to win the third set, who knows how the weekend might have been different? And if Coria had made something of his 3–1 and 5–3 leads in the first set of his rubber with Hrbaty, a dramatic final day turnaround would not have been inconceivable. But apart from the Hrbaty-Nalbandian singles, every time a crucial stage arose, the Slovaks always came out on top.

"I think we were a little unlucky," said Mancini on the Sunday night, trying to explain why Argentina had lost three semifinals and one quarterfinal in the previous four years. "We've had a lot of away draws, and Slovak Republic made the most of the choice of surface. If we had taken the first set of the doubles, or of either of Guillermo's singles, things might have been very different."

Though the three matches the Slovak Republic won were in straight sets, none was an emphatic win. Coria certainly had the better of the first set of the opening rubber against Beck, but couldn't make it count. The moment for doing so came in the tenth game of the first set, when Coria led 5–4 and had Beck at 0–30 on his serve. The cat seemed ready to pounce, but instead Beck reeled off twelve straight points, including two Coria double-faults in the eleventh game, and a set that seemed to be Coria's was suddenly in Beck's pocket.

Two nights before, the two players had seemed to be tussling over a beautiful woman. They weren't; it was all part of a colorful spectacle at the Semifinal's official dinner in which a renowned singer, Sisa Sklovska, contrived to let Coria pull off her wraparound skirt, and seconds later was dancing with Beck in front of the Argentinean team. Yet that proved something of a metaphor for the entire match. Beck, conceding forty ranking places to his more illustrious opponent, stole the admiration with a superb performance that saw him hold every service game and break Coria three times, which was enough for a 7–5 6–4 6–4 win.

Step one of the Slovak plan was complete, and the "third point from somewhere else" seemed to be on its way when Hrbaty led Nalbandian by a set and then led 15–40 on the

Pictured from top:

Guillermo Coria (ARG) found it a frustrating weekend;
Karol Beck played superbly for the Slovaks

Argentinean's serve at 5–5 in the second set. Two solid points allowed Nalbandian to save them, and then in the next game he found himself at set point. He decided to take a chance, and ended up hitting a stunning forehand return winner to level the match.

"I thought he was going to serve down the T, down the middle, and I was going there, but the serve was so good." Nalbandian said. "And I just caught it on the end of my racket, and the ball was so good. The game changed on my side, and I started playing better, and it was an incredible match."

Indeed it seemed it might be the turning point of the entire weekend, as Nalbandian won 3–6 7–5 7–5 6–3 to leave the first day level at 1–1. The visitors had had their shock, the talismanic Nalbandian had turned it around to extend to nine matches an unbeaten run in Davis Cup that stretched back to his debut in September 2002, and now the wind seemed to be in Argentina's sails. But the wind changed direction at the end of the first set of the doubles.

Nalbandian and Puerta went into Saturday's action as distinct favorites against Beck and Michal Mertinak. And while Nalbandian looked sluggish in the early exchanges, Puerta was everywhere, hitting some sizzling groundstrokes and making his presence felt at the net. But just as in Coria's match the previous day, they couldn't make it count. Beck and Mertinak served solidly, the set went to a tiebreak, and when the Argentineans lost the first four points of the tiebreak, it left them too much ground to make up as the Slovak Republic took the breaker 7–5.

That freed up the home pair and demoralized the visitors, allowing the Slovaks to take the second set. Puerta's high level dropped, and while the third set went to a second tiebreak, Nalbandian faced break points on all three of his service games. Again the Slovaks won the first four points of the breaker, leaving the Argentineans with a massive deficit to overhaul. At 6–2 Slovak Republic had four match points. Puerta saved the first with an ace and the second with one of his best returns of the afternoon off a superb Beck serve. Beck then double-faulted to make it 6–5. One more match point, but this time on the Nalbandian serve. The serve was good, and Puerta moved across to intercept the volley and played it firmly down at Mertinak's feet. But the Slovak reacted with an astonishing reflex half-volley that left Nalbandian stranded, and the rubber was over. A little bit of luck perhaps, but it was easy to feel the home pair had earned it.

Overnight a rumor circulated in Argentina that Gaudio would come in for Coria in the first reverse singles. There was never any truth to it, and Coria had been told on Friday night he would play Sunday's first match. When he hit two big forehands on the first point of his match against Hrbaty, he had signalled his intent to lay the foundations for a great final-day comeback. In a set of outstanding quality, Coria was the more imaginative, throwing in occasional drop shots to break up the relentless accuracy of Hrbaty's flat groundstrokes. Coria broke in the third and seventh games, and at 5–4 served for the set, but Hrbaty kept up a phenomenal level from the baseline and broke back twice. The first five points of the tiebreak went with serve, but at 3–2 Hrbaty broke free and was never behind after that.

He broke Coria twice in the second set and twice in the third. Only within sight of his historic victory did he wobble, some nervous shots allowing Coria to reach 15–40 at 4–3 to Hrbaty. But Hrbaty delivered four unreturnable serves to lead 5–3, and then broke to love, a Coria forehand finding the net to unleash wild celebrations in the Sibamac Arena.

Pictured from top:

Karol Beck (SVK) shows how much the tie mattered to him;
David Nalbandian (ARG) does likewise

Pictured opposite:

Dominik Hrbaty, for so long the standard bearer of Slovak tennis, scored the point which took his nation to the Final

SLOVAK REPUBLIC v ARGENTINA CONTINUED

After a lap of honor with the Slovak flag and a round of throwing all four players in the air, the Slovaks unveiled a banner that read in Spanish and Slovak: "Argentina you are fantastic. Thank you. Slovak fans."

Once the home fans saw the banner, they started to shout "Argentina, Argentina," and the visiting fans replied "Slovakia, Slovakia." The Argentinean fans even took the banner home with them, and it appeared in various media in Argentina.

Peter Kurhajec, the uncle of Slovak tennis player Lubomira Kurhajcova, is a big tennis fan and he had the banner made. "The atmosphere was just excellent. The Argentinean fans traveled a long journey to Slovakia and I wanted to express my respect to them and also to the Slovak fans that were great," he said.

It was a heartwarming gesture that typified the spirit of the tie, and it was a lot more aesthetically pleasing than the sight of all four Slovak team members with shaved heads—the result of a bet made in New York during the US Open. The general secretary of the Slovak Tennis Association, Igor Moska, did not escape either, but one member of the Slovak squad did¬—Captain Miloslav Mecir. Claiming that he had never agreed to the bet, he carried around an ice hockey helmet in his bag for protection, which he even brought to the post-tie party. ●

CROATIA v RUSSIA

In many ways the two semifinals were very similar. Both were hosted by young nations who had emerged from the post-Soviet era in eastern Europe, and who were in their first Davis Cup by BNP Paribas Semifinals. Both took place in compact stadiums in which passionate crowds of just a few thousand made the kind of noise you'd expect from much larger crowds. Both were played indoors when having a crystal ball a few weeks in advance would have allowed them to be played in glorious early autumn sunshine. And both were won by the home team in the fourth rubber after the first day's singles had been shared. But the big difference was that Russia put up a vastly better showing than Argentina, and came very close to spoiling Croatia's party.

Split may be Croatia's second city after the capital, Zagreb, but it is regarded as the nation's sporting center. The city is stunningly beautiful. It has the Mosor Kozjak Mountains as a backdrop, and spills down toward the waters of the Adriatic Sea, which appear turquoise in the summer sunshine. The city features in professionally made tourist videos, but any amateur movie footage shot on a sunny day in Split serves as an advertisement for this jewel of the Mediterranean.

The city, which has such a depth of history it celebrated its seventeen hundredth anniversary in 2005, is also the home of four of Croatia's greatest tennis players: Zeljko Franulovic, Niki Pilic, Goran Ivanisevic, and Mario Ancic (in fact they grew up in houses about one hundred meters from each other). And three of the four were involved in Croatia's greatest-ever tennis event on home soil: Ancic as a player, Pilic as captain, and Ivanisevic as coach. Ivanisevic deliberately missed the draw ceremony—such is his celebrity status following his 2001 Wimbledon triumph that his presence might well have

Pictured opposite from top:

Mariano Puerta and David Nalbandian (ARG) couldn't find the right answers in the doubles; the Slovak team celebrated wildly

Pictured from top:

Mario Ancic's disappointing Davis Cup singles run for Croatia continued; Nikolay Davydenko (RUS) is congratulated for keeping up his good 2005 form

CROATIA v RUSSIA CONTINUED

overshadowed the players, and he was keen to avoid that. But the weekend ended with Ivanisevic once again the story, as Pilic indicated the door was open for him to become Croatia's fourth player in the Final.

The reason Ivanisevic was keen to stay in the background was that Ivan Ljubicic was Croatia's true hero in 2005. For the third tie running, Ljubicic won both his singles and the doubles with Ancic, to see Croatia through—the first time this had been achieved since 1982, when John McEnroe also won nine out of nine rubbers through the semifinals. Ljubicic's win over Nikolay Davydenko also took his unbeaten run in Davis Cup to eleven matches.

But to keep his record intact, Ljubicic needed his third and fourth five-setters of the year. And as in the quarterfinals, he needed to steady the Croatian ship after Ancic had lost the opening rubber to a very sharp Davydenko.

For the visitors, the ideal scenario would have been to have Marat Safin playing Ancic and Davydenko facing Ljubicic. But the Australian Open champion was still resting his troublesome knee and was never seriously expected to play. That meant it was always going to be tough for the visitors against a team who had the luxury of keeping the big-serving Ivo Karlovic in reserve. Davydenko did what was needed from him on the opening day, using his big forehand to beat Ancic 7–5 6–4 5–7 6–4. The Russian will feel it should have been three sets—he served for the match at 5–4 in the third, only to lose the next three games as Ancic was finally able to mobilize the passionate support in the Sportski Centar Gripe. But the Russian regrouped in the fourth to continue a poor year in singles for Ancic.

Up stepped Ljubicic, but for large stretches of his match against Mikhail Youzhny, there was a real possibility that Russia would end the first day two points up. Youzhny took the first set as Ljubicic was slow to start, but once the Croat had broken in the second game of the second set, it opened the gates to some of his best form. He had chances to go up a break in the fourth, but when they went begging and Youzhny got the break, the match was headed for a cliff-hanging fifth set.

The fifth game was the decisive one. Youzhny saved several break points as the crowd tried to encourage their man with ear-splitting noise. The tennis was at times outstanding, as the quality matched the drama. One point saw Youzhny diving for a volley, making it, but lying helpless on the floor as Ljubicic raced to put the ball into an open court.

"I felt I had to do something special to break him," said Ljubicic afterward, "and I did."

Ljubicic finally got his break, and with his serve working superbly all day, that was all that was needed to secure a 3–6 6–3 6–4 4–6 6–4 victory in three hours and three minutes.

The opening singles in Split had indeed been split, but if Croatia's fans thought that win had broken Russia's resistance, they were in for a shock on the Saturday. The five sets had taken a lot out of Youzhny, so Russia's captain Shamil Tarpiishev used his third different doubles team of the year in picking Igor Andreev to partner the Davis Cup debutant, Dmitry Tursunov, against Ancic and Ljubicic. And for the second day running, Ljubicic had to go the full distance in a match that exceeded the previous day's offering for passion and drama.

Croatia took both Tursunov's opening service games for a comfortable first set, but Ancic was broken twice early in the second as Russia leveled. The third set had the lion's share of the drama, most notably when a dashing pass by Tursunov was called "in" when most of the home supporters had seen it wide. The already vociferous crowd went wild, and after

Pictured opposite from top:
Ivan Ljubicic (CRO) was focused on winning for his country; he celebrated each point with his teammates
Pictured from top:
Mikhail Youzhny (RUS) pushed Ljubicic all the way; Dmitry Tursunov (left) and Igor Andreev battled bravely for Russia in the doubles

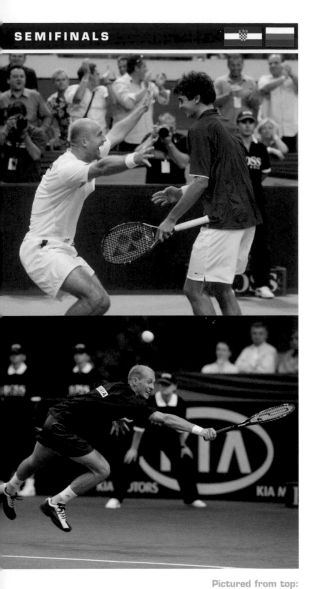

Pictured from top:

Ivan Ljubicic and Mario Ancic (CRO) had the midas
touch in the doubles yet again; Nikolay Davydenko (RUS)
gave his all but it wasn't enough against Ljubicic

Pictured opposite from top:

Ivan ljubicic (CRO) and his wife Aida; Ljubicic enjoyed
some more raucous celebrations with his teammates

CROATIA v RUSSIA CONTINUED

making their own protests to umpire Carlos Ramos and referee Sören Friemel, Ancic and
Ljubicic had to exercise some semaphore skills by waving to their fans to calm down. There
was a serious danger that Croatia might be penalized under the "partisan crowd" rule.

The crowd eventually accepted the situation but were preparing to mourn when
Russia opened up a 5–2 lead in the third set tiebreak. Yet the Croatian pair reeled off five
straight points, culminating in a delicately angled Ljubicic volley on set point, to send the
noise level even higher than it had been to date—if that was possible.

But back bounced the Russians. A break in the second game of the fourth set sufficed
to take the match into a decider. The Croats had the benefit of serving first, and that
advantage told when Andreev served to stay in the match at 4–5. On match point
Tursunov missed a volley, and after three hours and 37 minutes, the scoreboard read 6–2
4–6 7–6(5) 3–6 6–4 for the home side.

Though the home team had the momentum, Ljubicic had played ten sets in two days
and had to open on the final day against Davydenko, the man who had played brilliantly
on the last day of the quarterfinals to beat France's Richard Gasquet. What would have
happened if Davydenko had broken back at 3–5 in the first set or had capitalized on his 5–3
lead in the second-set tiebreak will never be known. But Ljubicic won all the important
points, and the adrenaline rush was sufficient to keep all hints of tiredness at bay.

He faced break points early in the third set, but his serving was superb all weekend and
he kept on level terms. Then with Davydenko serving at 4–5 to stay in the match, Ljubicic
found another gear. On match point he crunched a forehand down the line, the stadium
erupted, and within minutes forty-five hundred joyous Croats were dancing in the aisles.

"It is unbelievable really," said Ljubcic later, his voice breaking with emotion. "From
the first moment I played Davis Cup I wanted to win one match, win one by one, and
we've gone through to the Final. This is a historic performance. I can't put this into words.
Maybe tomorrow when I calm down a bit but this crowd is incredible. Not one single
person left the stadium even an hour after we finished. It's unbelievable!"

If the wider tennis world felt the 2005 Davis Cup by BNP Paribas Final would involve
two teams without any household names, Croatia's captain Niki Pilic suggested in his
team's post-tie press conference that this might not be the case. With Ancic, Ljubicic, and
Karlovic guaranteed a berth for the final, the question of Croatia's fourth player arose.

The obvious candidates were Roko Karanusic or Sasa Tuskar, but Pilic suggested that
Ivanisevic—for so long the flag-bearer of Croatian tennis, indeed of Croatia as a nation—
might find his way into the lineup for the Final. The legend, a mere thirty-four years old,
had been playing on the seniors' tour, and Pilic offered him a play-off match with Tuskar
to decide the fourth member of the team for the final. Whether it was meant seriously,
no one could judge at the time, but it added another human element to an already highly
emotional moment in the development of the young Adriatic nation.

With the Sportski Centar Gripe finally empty, a wag in the scoreboard cabin decided
to have some fun. On the big electronic board, he put up the words "Davis Cup by BNP
Paribas Final—Croatia 5, Slovak Republic 0."

That was highly unlikely to happen, but it was a sign of the self-confidence of this
still teenage nation. ●

THEATRES OF DREAMS

One of the beauties of the Davis Cup is that it visits many different countries and many different types of venue each year.
Here are just some of the colorful, crazy and breathtaking arenas in which the great competition has unfolded in 2005.

Name

DOMINIK HRBATY

Born

JANUARY 4, 1978,
IN BRATISLAVA,
SLOVAK REPUBLIC

Turned professional

1996

Dominik Hrbaty has long been a standard-bearer for Slovak tennis, and appropriately enough he was the hero as he took the point that sent his nation through to its first-ever Final.

PLAYER OF THE ROUND

IN JANUARY 1997, PETE Sampras was on top of the world. Despite the spirited challenge of Andre Agassi in 1995, he had finished the previous four years at the top of the rankings and was at the height of his powers. His route to a second Australian Open title seemed moderately easy, but then in the fourth round, he came up against a nineteen-year-old who seemed to have lost a vowel in his surname.

Dominik Hrbaty (pronounced "her-bátty"), a smiling, happy-go-lucky Slovak, had the great man on the run. He took Sampras to a final set and led 4–2, even having a break point for 5–2. In the end Sampras used his experience to snuff out the young challenge, but Hrbaty had made his mark. And when he reached the Roland Garros semifinals two years later, losing to Agassi, he seemed to have arrived as a force at the top of men's tennis.

Set against that background, the middle part of Hrbaty's career seems a shade disappointing. He drifted out of the top 50 in 2002 and 2003, and while he bounced back in 2004 to reach a career-high ranking of No. 12, his impressive form on the ATP circuit contrasted with a somewhat disappointing year in the Grand Slams. It created a sense of promise unfulfilled.

Somewhere along the line, he picked up the rather inappropriate nickname "the Dominator." It's inappropriate because, unlike most players, Hrbaty doesn't seek to dominate, only to win. He is understated, interested in sport in general more than specifically tennis (at eleven he had to choose between skiing and tennis; he's into mountain biking, deep-sea fishing and supreme fitness, and he hopes one day to run the New York marathon), and has tended to view all matches as being of equal importance, whether at Slams, tour events, or even Challenger level. The sparkling eyes and love of fun tend to shine through an essentially shy exterior, such that you almost get the impression he's happiest just behind the tier of tennis superstars who attract more attention than he himself would be comfortable with.

Growing up in what was then Czechoslovakia, his idol was Ivan Lendl, who hailed from Ostrava, just two hundred kilometers from Hrbaty's home in the Slovak capital Bratislava. The two play similar games, based around attacking power from the baseline. But Hrbaty's ambition is more contained than Lendl's. In 2001 he told the French sports daily L'Équipe: "I don't want to set any goals that are too high, because I'm progressing little by little, and there are plenty of great players at the big tournaments. Every day I'm learning lots of new things, so everything in its own time."

And if Slovak Republic's superb Davis Cup run in 2005 proves the high point of Hrbaty's career, then everything will have built up, little by little, to its climax at age twenty-seven. True, both Hrbaty and his country had some luck in 2005, notably with four home ties. And for Hrbaty they really were home: his father, an architectural engineer, owns the hotel built onto the side of the National Tennis Centre that hosted all of the Slovak Republic's Davis Cup matches in 2005, so Dominik was able to wander in and out, grabbing an apple or a bowl of pasta when the mood took him.

But this is not a shrinking violet who is just happy to play his matches and then disappear. In 2001 his face was all over Slovak Republic as part of an anti-drugs campaign that he supported, and he's very much a hands-on idol in his country. In a small and still young country, Dominik Hrbaty is a national treasure—recognized more at home sometimes than on the international tennis circuit. ●

play-off ties 23–25 SEPTEMBER

Spain defeated Italy 3–2   TORRE DEL GRECO, ITALY—OUTDOOR CLAY

Germany defeated Czech Repubic 3–2   LIBEREC, CZECH REPUBLIC—INDOOR CLAY

Switzerland defeated Great Britain 5–0   GENEVA, SWITZERLAND—INDOOR CLAY

USA defeated Belgium 4–1   LEUVEN, BELGIUM—INDOOR CLAY

Sweden defeated India 3–1   NEW DELHI, INDIA—OUTDOOR GRASS

Austria defeated Ecuador 4–1   PORTSCHACH, AUSTRIA—OUTDOOR HARD

Belarus defeated Canada 3–2   TORONTO, CANADA—OUTDOOR HARD

Chile defeated Pakistan 5–0   SANTIAGO, CHILE—OUTDOOR CLAY

Getronics

ICT SOLUTIONS AND SERVICES

PLAY-OFF TIES

THE TWENTY-FIFTH PLAY-OFF ties proved to be one of the most high-quality sets of these ties since the World Group was established in 1981. Both the previous year's finalists, Spain and the USA, figured in the eight ties, as did the world Nos. 1, 2, and 4. It was also a round in which three players came back from two sets to love down to win in five—but all three ended up on the losing side! ●

ITALY v SPAIN

IN AD 79, THE VOLCANO Mount Vesuvius in what today is southern Italy erupted, dumping its red-hot lava over the ancient city of Pompeii. In 2005, the Italian Tennis Association took its seemingly hopeless Davis Cup Play-off tie against the mighty Spain to Torre del Greco in the foothills of Mount Vesuvius. Despite the loss of Italy's top-ranked player, Filippo Volandri, due to a contractual dispute, and the local hero Potito Starace to flu, Italy's tennis players and crowd erupted and very nearly created their own piece of history.

Though impressive on paper, Spain was heavily reliant on its 2005 red-hot tennis sensation, Rafael Nadal. The nineteen-year-old was scheduled to play on all three days, and coming from winning his tenth title of the year in Beijing the previous weekend, the workload almost caught up with him on the final day. His two singles wins were needed, after another example of how Juan Carlos Ferrero was still struggling to rediscover the form that took him to the top of the rankings in 2003.

Ferrero suffered chickenpox in early 2004, and then had wrist and rib injuries. It not only meant a slump in the rankings, but he lost the air of invincibility that he had had in winning Roland Garros in 2003. In countless matches he would open up a lead, only to find he couldn't finish the job.

So when Ferrero led Andreas Seppi by two sets to love in the opening rubber, nothing was settled for sure. Despite conceding fifty-eight ranking places, Seppi knew it, and stormed back to take the third set. The fourth was competitive, but once Seppi had taken it, Ferrero looked a tired figure and Italy took a 1–0 lead.

Nadal's straight-sets win over Daniele Bracciali, who came in for Starace (who himself had come in for Volandri), leveled the scores, but Spain once again showed they have not resolved their doubles problem. Nadal and Feliciano Lopez are good friends and formed a useful all-left-handed partnership. But they were beaten 9–7 by Daniele Bracciali and Giorgio Galimberti in the fifth set of a four-hour, thirty-seven-minute thriller, to leave Italy on the verge of ending its five-year exile from the World Group and placing Spain in danger of becoming only the third nation to exit the elite division in the year after winning the cup.

On the final day, Nadal won the first two sets against Seppi with near-perfect tennis, but the court time and travel began to catch up with him in the third, which Seppi won 7–5. What would have happened if Seppi hadn't faltered to allow Nadal to win the fourth 6–4 will never be known, but Nadal's work was over, the tie was 2–2, and Spain's hopes rested with Ferrero.

How Corrado Barrazutti would have loved to have had the accomplished Volandri, or even the local boy Starace, to throw in. But he had to stick to the tiring Bracciali, who

Pictured from top:

Andreas Seppi (ITA) scored a great win over Juan Carlos Ferrero (ESP); Ferrero's 2005 woes continued on the opening day; friends Rafael Nadal (left) and Feliciano Lopez formed the Spanish doubles pairing

Pictured opposite from top:

Giorgio Galimberti (left) and Daniele Bracciali scored a tremendous win in the doubles for Italy; Rafael Nadal (ESP)

couldn't build on his doubles win, as Ferrero rang up a two sets lead. Buoyed by the way Seppi had won, Bracciali fought back in the third, but Ferrero wasn't going to let two fish get away in the same weekend, and ensured that Spain stayed up with a relatively comfortable win.

The French, who won so ecstatically in Malmö in 1996, went down the following year, and Sweden, winners within two days against Italy in the 1998 Final, couldn't stay up in '99. Spain came close to joining them but ultimately staved off defeat to remain one of the favorites for 2006. ●

CZECH REPUBLIC v
GERMANY

HISTORY WAS MADE IN Liberec, when the World Group's longest consistent run ended in the closest of the eight Play-off ties.

When it came into existence in 1993, the Czech Republic took Czechoslovakia's place in the elite division. Czechoslovakia had been there for twelve years, since the World Group began in 1981, and the smaller Czech Republic notched up thirteen years of its own. But on a slow, damp clay court that saw twenty-three sets lasting eighteen hours and twenty-five minutes, the irresistible force behind a full-strength German team—looking to return to the World Group for the first time in three years—proved too strong for the immovable Czech object, and the Czechs went into the Europe/Africa Zone for the first time.

"Germany is back where it belongs," said Tommy Haas after a marathon weekend for him—fourteen sets over ten hours twenty-six minutes. And Germany's captain, Patrik Kühnen, said his countryfolk were expecting at least a semifinal or even a final in 2006 if they got a good first-round draw. Such is the optimism of the nation that won the Davis Cup three times: as West Germany in 1988 and '89 when Boris Becker was in his prime, and again as a united Germany in 1993 in Michael Stich's best year. But it had taken Kühnen, the softly spoken doubles partner of both Becker and Stich, quite a while to get all the forces of the post-Becker and Stich era together. Now he had them in the same place at the same time, and Germany was to prove too strong for a Czech team lacking the injured Jiri Novak.

The first day had more action than some ties that are decided in two days. The Czechs' No. 1 player, Tomas Berdych, came back from two sets down to beat Haas, surviving three match points in a most dramatic fourth-set tiebreak that the Czech won 11–9. Haas led 2–0 in the final set, but when Berdych came back to win it 6–3, he hailed it as the best win of his career, even better than his landmark win over Roger Federer at the 2004 Athens Olympic Games.

Nicolas Kiefer came back from dropping the second set to beat Tomas Zib in four, and when Haas and the doubles specialist Alexander Waske gave Germany a 2–1 lead in a three-hour, thirty-eight-minute five-setter against the doubles specialists and Davis Cup

Pictured opposite top to bottom:
Patrik Kühnen (left) and the German bench were vociferous throughout; Kühnen celebrates victory in the doubles with Tommy Haas and Alexander Waske (facing)
Pictured from top:
Tommy Haas (GER) (left) and Tomas Berdych (CZE) had a fierce battle; Berdych is encouraged by Czech Captain Cyril Suk

Pictured from top:

Great Britain Captain Jeremy Bates opted to gamble with his selections, but ultimately it didn't pay off; rising star Andrew Murray (GBR) suffered one of the few setbacks of an impressive debut year

Pictured opposite from top:

Roger Federer (SUI) (right) easily disposed of Alan Mackin (GBR); the Swiss team were relieved to secure another year in the World Group

debutants Frantisek Cermak and Leos Friedl, anyone would have thought Germany had won the entire competition. The celebrations following Waske's forehand crosscourt return that won Germany the match were so emotional that even the mild-mannered Kühnen couldn't resist racing onto the court and jumping to embrace his players, who had just notched up their third successive five-set win in Davis Cup. The message was clear: Germany had won the most important point of the weekend.

But the weekend was to bring several more twists; indeed, seldom can a day's Davis Cup by BNP Paribas play have been so exciting as the Sunday in the Arena Liberec. Twice Kiefer led Berdych by a set. Twice Berdych came back. The twenty-year-old Czech had won all his four five-set matches, but the latest was only two days earlier—surely tiredness would work in Kiefer's favor. But at 5–5, Kiefer was broken to love, Berdych served out the victory, and the tie that seemed heading westward to Germany was back level at 2–2.

With Zib leading Haas by 7–6, 4–1, the momentum was definitely heading eastward, Haas in his twelfth set of the weekend looked exhausted, and the Germans' dream team was heading for defeat. But one break turned the match around. Haas broke back in the seventh game, broke again in the eleventh, and suddenly the deciding rubber stood at a set all. From then on, Zib faded badly, Haas went from strength to strength, and in the end it was a somewhat anticlimactic end to a weekend of such drama.

A young German team it was not. But after several years in which Haas, Kiefer, and Rainer Schüttler all hit their individual best in the absence of their compatriots, Kühnen had finally got them—together with the doubles specialist Waske—playing together and passionate about winning for their country. Four days later, Kühnen got his wish for a reasonable draw for the 2006 World Group first round—another "away" tie just across the border, this time to the west in France. The Germans were back! ●

SWITZERLAND v
GREAT BRITAIN

THE DAVIS CUP BY BNP Paribas rulebook was stretched to its limit in the tactical machinations that led up to this ultimately one-sided tie.

With Roger Federer back for Switzerland and in such imperious form, Great Britain's captain, Jeremy Bates, made a simple calculation: his team's only chance of winning was to beat Switzerland's No. 2, Stanislas Wawrinka, twice and win the doubles. So his entire strategy was built around that. It certainly took the Swiss by surprise. Federer admitted after the draw that he was slightly taken aback at having to face not the brave new face of British tennis, Andy Murray, but the 262nd-ranked Alan Mackin on the opening day. This was because Bates figured Murray would have a fair chance of beating Wawrinka. He might also have opted for Greg Rusedski against Wawrinka but wanted to save Murray's energy for just two matches, so he decided not to throw him in against Federer on the opening day.

Pictured from top:

Olivier Rochus (BEL) scored an impressive win over James Blake;

Blake (USA) couldn't bring his hard-court form to the clay in Belgium;

the Bryan brothers once again came up trumps for USA

The result was an opening rubber in which Mackin was thrown to the lions and escaped having won two games against the great Federer. And then Wawrinka and Murray played in the match that would determine whether the British had a chance or not. If Wawrinka was taken by surprise having prepared for a big-serving left-hander, only to face a solid right-hander with a rapidly rising profile in men's tennis, he certainly didn't show it. He raced to a 5–1 lead as Murray seemed slow to get his racket out of his bag.

But from then on, Murray—an eighteen-year-old from Scotland playing his first Davis Cup singles rubber—showed he was Wawrinka's equal by getting one of the breaks back and then matching the Swiss game for game in the second set. With Murray leading 4–1 in the second-set tiebreak, things looked good for the Briton. But from 3–5 down, Wawrinka won four points on the run to take the second set. Murray's frustration in going back to his chair after losing the tiebreak was evident, for there in the space of four points went Great Britain's hopes of taking something out of the weekend. Though Murray broke early in the third set, he was broken twice as Wawrinka notched up his first live Davis Cup win.

Though the doubles was competitive, and the British pair of Rusedski and Murray won a set against Federer and Yves Allegro, the sting had gone out of the weekend. Even if the British had won—and the first-time pairing seemed a genuinely capable underdog— the chances of Murray beating Federer on the following day were so remote that the tie was won and lost. In the end, it was sealed with a four-sets win for the Swiss in the doubles, and with the two dead rubbers played by second-string players going to the Swiss, Bates's sensible gamble turned into a 5–0 defeat.

For the home nation, it was a sign of what could be possible with Federer now supported by a confident second-singles player. Wawrinka proved as much the key to the Swiss success as the world No. 1, and his progress would hold the key to Switzerland's hopes in 2006. For the British, the tie came two weeks too early—a week later Murray reached his first ATP final, losing a tight two-setter to Federer in Bangkok. With that run of confidence behind him, he might have carried greater weight in his singles with Wawrinka. ●

BELGIUM v USA

IN THE COURSE OF an average year, tennis fans regularly have cause to glance at the word "Leuven." The university city just east of Brussels is home to one of Belgium's most famous trademarks, the Stella Artois brewery, sponsors of the pre-Wimbledon grass court tournament at London's Queen's club. And "Leuven" appears on the red label of the beer that prides itself on being expensive.

Leuven now also appears on the tennis records of Andy Roddick, James Blake, and the Bryan twins, after Patrick McEnroe's USA team survived a long and ultimately controversial battle brewed over three absorbing days and served up on the clay of a converted basketball arena. During the warm-up to the weekend, Andy Roddick was honored by the Davis Cup sponsor Getronics for his three world speed service records in 2004, but it was one of the smallest players on the circuit who threatened to steal the limelight.

Olivier Rochus is just one meter 65, or five feet, five inches. Like other diminutive names from tennis's recent past (Michael Chang, Alberto Berasategui, Jaime Yzaga to name three), he has to make up with speed and guile what he lacks in reach. By September 2005 he was into the world's Top 30 and almost took a set off Roger Federer— his doubles partner from junior days—at the US Open.

In front of his home crowd, Rochus played one of the weekends of his life. But he was ultimately left on the losing side, at least in part by an unfortunate line call that so soured the end of the superb Rochus-Roddick match that the Americans felt it best to mute their celebrations at staying in the World Group. At least Rochus has the satisfaction of knowing he took the 2004 runners-up to the limit, and posted Belgium's one win of the weekend.

That was against James Blake in the opening rubber. Blake, whose superb run on the American hard courts earned him a recall to his beloved Davis Cup for the first time in two years, was left scratching his head at Rochus's phenomenal retrieving ability. It wore away at his confidence on serve, and the match ended on the American's seventh double fault, though the damage had been done much earlier.

Roddick quickly righted the U.S. ship with a straight-sets win over Rochus's elder (and slightly taller) brother, Christophe, before the Americans cashed in the one point they were fairly certain of, the doubles. The Belgians have had problems finding a reliable doubles pair for years, while Bob and Mike Bryan brought to Leuven a record of five wins in six rubbers. Though they were fully respectful of the Olivier Rochus and Kristof Vliegen partnership—Rochus and Xavier Malisse had won the 2004 Roland Garros doubles title— their class was always going to be too much for the home pair. The four-sets victory testifies to how persistent the Belgian duo was—one American journalist described them as being "like gnats on a mid-summer picnic: they annoy, gosh do they annoy, but they do not stop the fun"—but the outcome was never seriously in doubt.

That set the stage for the epic four-hour, thirty-two-minute Rochus-Roddick match. Roddick has worked hard on his clay court game, and while it will never be his favorite surface, his big serve makes him a useful performer. Yet he was like a runner who couldn't get away from the pack. Whenever he got ahead, Rochus clawed his way back. The first three sets were tiebreaks, and when Roddick took the third for a 2–1 lead, Rochus might easily have wilted. But wilting isn't in the Belgian's vocabulary, and he bounced back to take the fourth.

In the sixth game of the final set, the drama happened. Leading 3–2, Roddick had two break points. Rochus attacked with a forehand, Roddick threw up a lob, Rochus smashed crosscourt—one break point saved. But no. McEnroe saw the line judge put out her hand and drew this to the attention of the umpire, Sune Alenkaer. He consulted the lineswoman, who confirmed she had called the smash out. Players and officials looked for a mark, but none could be found. In such circumstances the umpire has to go with the original call, which was "out," so he called "game: USA." Cue the first ill-tempered booing from the passionate but hitherto fair and respectful crowd in the Leuven Sportplaza.

"The ball was not even touching the line," Rochus said later. "The umpire was so sure it was good he didn't even see the mark. I don't know how the lineswoman could see it out."

Pictured from top:
A disputed line-call stole many of the headlines;
Olivier Rochus (BEL) was bitterly disappointed to be
on the losing side

It's possible Roddick would have won anyway. He had a second break point, and he was serving well in the final set. But when, a mere three games later, he sealed the USA's place in the 2006 World Group, there were no mass celebrations, either by him or his teammates.

"To be honest, after what happened, it would have been unprofessional to go on and on," Roddick explained. "The team came on court, but I said, 'Let's get out of here.' It wouldn't be right [to celebrate on court], especially because you don't want a match of that quality to end like that. If we celebrate as a team in a small room, then we do. But I didn't feel that was the right time or place to go on."

So for the third year, Belgium lost in the Play-offs, and Rochus felt he lost it on a call that few heard and for which no mark in the clay could be found.

"I never played a match that was so close," he said disbelievingly. "To go out like this is tough. What can you do?" Answer: come back next year and try again. And at twenty-four, Rochus still has time on his side. ●

INDIA v SWEDEN

MANY A TEAM HAS sweated and stumbled in the humid heat of India. The Netherlands and Switzerland both took highly regarded teams to the subcontinent in the 1990s only to come away defeated, and India's run to the 1987 Davis Cup Final involved victories at home over Argentina and Israel.

But fielding a team of two singles players whose experience is largely from the Challenger circuit, India came up against a Swedish lineup populated with players determined to prove that their best days were not behind them. In the end there were two winners: Sweden and the rain, the visitors finally sealing their place in the World Group on the fourth day of competition with the fifth rubber unable to be played.

Indeed, by the time Thomas Johansson gave Sweden a 2–0 lead, it was late afternoon on Sunday. Jonas Björkman had given the visitors the early advantage with a straight-sets win over Prakash Amritraj, whose father, Vijay, had played singles and doubles in the 1987 Final away to Sweden. But after an early end on Friday and a day's fruitless waiting on Saturday, followed by a delay on Sunday while a corner of the grass court dried out, Johansson and Rohan Bhopanna finally managed to resume their second singles at 3:30 p.m. on the third day of the tie. Johansson went on to win on three tiebreaks, after saving two set points in the third set.

Bad light caused the doubles to be halted after Björkman and Simon Aspelin had taken the first set against India's experienced Leander Paes and Mahesh Bhupathi. When they resumed on the Monday in stifling heat, the Indian pair edged out the world No. 1 (Björkman) and 20 (Aspelin) to win in four sets and post India's first live victory over Sweden in more than twenty years. With the ball keeping low, Aspelin's timing disintegrated, while Björkman—perhaps with an eye on a possible live singles later in the day—seemed to have less than his usual vibrant energy.

But with Johansson in good form, it would have been a surprise for India to have won

Pictured from top:

Jürgen Melzer (AUT); Stefan Koubek (AUT) let slip his rubber
against Nicolas Lapentti; the Austria team rightly applauded
Jürgen Melzer as their hero of the weekend

the fourth rubber, and the Swede—who has won grass-court titles in Halle and Nottingham, and was a semifinalist at Wimbledon eleven weeks earlier—ran out a straight-sets winner against Amritraj, to leave the final score 3–1 (the fifth rubber wasn't played).

The big loser of the weekend was the court, which was described by Johansson as "the worst grass court I've ever played on." Perhaps because of that, there was some relief for the Swedish captain Mats Wilander, as victory allowed him to prepare for an eighth Davis Cup triumph in 2006.

"My boys take huge pride in playing the Davis Cup," he said after Johansson's win. "It doesn't matter if they have other engagements, Swedish tradition is such that they will play the Davis Cup." ●

AUSTRIA v ECUADOR

THE MOST ECSTATIC MOMENT in the recent tennis history of Ecuador came at Wimbledon in July 2000. Looking for its first year back in the Davis Cup World Group since a three-year run in the mid-1980s, the South American team traveled with little realistic hope to the new Court 1 at Wimbledon and beat a British team boasting Tim Henman and Greg Rusedski in a live fifth rubber.

The star of that win was Giovanni Lapentti, then just eighteen. His win from two sets down over Arvind Parmar—stepping in for the injured Rusedski—seemed to signal a great future for the younger of the two tennis-playing brothers. Only a year earlier, his elder brother, Nicolas, had been ranked in the world's Top Ten at the end of the best year of his career. The future for Ecuador looked bright.

But the elder Lapentti never reached those heights again, and the younger never built on his great success. Five years on, here were the brothers, singlehandedly carrying their country's hopes into another play-off round under the captaincy of Raul Viver, a survivor of Ecuador's time in the World Group in the 1980s. And Giovanni cut a sad figure in his thrashing in the opening rubber by Jürgen Melzer in Portschach. Ranked 133 to Melzer's 49th, Lapentti could have embraced the opportunity of taking on a beatable player having to deal with the pressure of home expectations. But he won just three games, constantly threw his racket, and was given two warnings by the umpire: one for racket abuse, the other for an audible obscenity.

When Stefan Koubek led Nicolas Lapentti by two sets to love, Ecuador's cause seemed lost. But the elder Lapentti always raises his level in Davis Cup by BNP Paribas and came back to post the third comeback from 0–2 in the eight Play-off ties. The crucial phase was the fourth-set tiebeak, when Koubek was in sight of victory, only for Lapentti to take it 7–5. Koubek got fresh impetus in the fifth set, but by then the momentum was with Lapentti, and in the twelfth game the Ecuadorian broke to decide the four-and-a-half hour match in his favor.

The result seemed to demoralize the Austrian camp, the home captain Thomas Muster saying: "We missed a big chance today." But though none of the Austrian players will ever reach the heights Muster scaled, they formed a team that had considerable depth. Because of Melzer's quick singles, he came in instead of Alexander Peya for the doubles to partner Julian Knowle in the Austrians' top combination. And though both Austrians were broken in the opening set, they managed to win the match in four.

The one source of hope for Ecuador was that Giovanni Lapentti would raise his level of play, and Viver said that if Nicolas could beat Jürgen Melzer in the first reverse singles—and he had beaten the Austrian in their two previous matches—he fancied Giovanni to beat Koubek in the decider.

But it was all wishful thinking. It was Melzer's weekend, and he wrapped up his and Austria's third point of the tie with a tight straight-sets win over the elder brother. Lapentti laid the platform for another come-from-behind win when he broke in the seventh game of the third set, but Melzer broke twice in Lapentti's next three service games to ensure Austria remained in the World Group for a third successive year. ●

CANADA v **BELARUS**

VLADIMIR VOLTCHKOV PUT HIS head on the block when he said to Canadian reporters after the doubles: "Tomorrow's a new day. Things will happen. I think you guys used your luck already in a very, very strong way these two days."

The normally shy twenty-seven-year-old from Minsk, whose form in Davis Cup always outstrips his disappointingly low ranking, could have been made to look a fool. He had after all just lost the doubles to see Canada go 2–1 up. But after his third victory in a live fifth rubber that saw Belarus retain its World Group status, he was proved right. Canada's luck, which had served it so well and seen the tie go through to 7 p.m. on the Sunday night, had finally run out.

For the hosts, the calculation was simple. Their top-ranked player, Frank Dancevic, had to beat Voltchkov on the opening day, they had to win the doubles, and they had to pick up one singles from somewhere else. And in a weekend of two five-setters and no straight-sets wins in the new Rexall Centre venue built for the Toronto Masters, it so nearly worked.

The question for Canada's captain Martin Laurendeau was whether to go for Daniel Nestor or Frederic Niemeyer for the opening day's singles. Either would start as underdog against Belarus's top player, Max Mirnyi, but if Dancevic were to play Voltchkov first and beat him, then who would have the best chance of capitalizing on the momentum and taking Mirnyi by surprise? Though the thirty-three-year-old Nestor hadn't played singles outside Davis Cup for over a year, he was given the nod.

The draw helped by putting the Dancevic-Voltchkov match first, Dancevic did his bit by winning, and at 7–6 5–2 to Nestor in the second rubber, Canada's master plan was working to perfection. But in the space of five games it unraveled. For nearly two sets Nestor showed some wonderful touch around the net, displaying the form that has seen him beat three former world No. 1 players (Edberg, Rios, and Kuerten) in a Davis Cup career going back to 1992. But serving for the second set at 5–3 he had two double

Pictured from top:

Vladimir Voltchkov (BLR) made some fiery comments to the press over the weekend; Frank Dancevic (CAN); Max Mirnyi (rear) and Voltchkov are a strong partnership for Belarus but lost in Toronto

Pictured from top:

Fernando Gonzalez (CHI); Aqeel Khan (PAK)

faults, was broken, and then missed four set points on Mirnyi's serve at 5–4. Another double fault contributed to Nestor losing his serve again, and minutes later Mirnyi had leveled the match. With Nestor then feeling a pain in his left hip and knowing he was needed for the doubles, he retired hurt at 1–2 in the third set.

That left the overnight score 1–1, but the visitors feeling the happier. Dancevic's superb five-set win over Voltchkov in a minute over four hours had been cancelled out, and both men were left tending the injuries that caused half a dozen treatments in the intense match.

Canada wasn't out of it; indeed, they held the upper hand after a four-sets victory by Nestor and Niemeyer over Mirnyi and Voltchkov in the doubles. The match was notable for an angry exchange between Mirnyi and the referee, Brian Earley, in the fourth set. The umpire, Jaime Chavez, denied Belarus a point after Mirnyi claimed in mid-rally that Niemeyer had hit the ball twice in one shot. As Chavez deemed Niemeyer's shot to be legal, he penalized Mirnyi under the "hindrance" rule. Mirnyi declined to blame Belarus's defeat on that one incident, but that—coupled with Nestor's announcement that he would not be playing singles—no doubt contributed to Voltchkov's belief that the Canadians had used up all their luck.

In a match delayed over an hour by rain, Dancevic defied his ranking of 188 to take the 27th-ranked Mirnyi to five sets. He also defied considerable pain, needing to leave the court for eight minutes to get treatment in the third set. With the level of serving getting better during the final set, it took just one break—in the last game of the match—for Mirnyi to wrap up victory, and both players left the court to warm applause.

That brought Voltchkov back for his third match of the weekend, with nine sets on his clock, and just eight ranking places above his opponent, Niemeyer. Voltchkov took the first set. Niemeyer then led 5–3 in the second, but after missing four set points he seemed to lose his way, as Voltchkov served for a two-sets lead at 6–5. But Niemeyer broke back, won the tiebreak 7–2, and gave the dwindling but enthusiastic home crowd renewed hope of a home win. But when Voltchkov played two superb points to break for 5–3 in the third set, he had taken a decisive lead, and one break in the fourth set sufficed to see Belarus home. ●

CHILE v PAKISTAN

THIS MAY HAVE BEEN the most one-sided of the eight Play-off ties, but it was also in some ways the most satisfying. The sheer fact that Pakistan was one tie away from reaching the World Group was a milestone in itself for the growth of tennis in countries that have little history of the sport.

Despite being a neighbor to India, whose tennis tradition goes back several decades, Pakistan has little history of producing top-class players, other than Iftikhar Ahmed, who served Pakistan well in Davis Cup in the 1950s and '60s, and Haroon Rahim, who reached a tour-level final in the 1970s (at Little Rock in 1977), won the doubles at the same event, and reached the quarterfinals of the doubles event at the 1971 US Open.

More recently, though, Aisam Qureshi made his mark as a doubles player. And he really made his mark! His partner at a run of Grand Slams was the Israeli Amir Hadad, which made for a Muslim-Jewish pairing at a time when antipathy between Arabs and Jews was hampering attempts to find peace in the Middle East. It wasn't the first time Qureshi had played with diplomatically sensitive opponents—he had played at satellite level with two other Israelis, Andy Ram and Noam Behr, and with two Indians, Harsh Mankad and Mustafa Ghouse—but his pairing with Hadad caught the imagination, especially when they won a few rounds. Qureshi comfortably parried the attacks from those who didn't like his choice of partner, but ploughed a largely lone furrow for Pakistan in international tennis.

But gradually, Pakistan made its mark. And in 2005 it celebrated wins over Thailand and Japan, which led to its first-ever tie not in the Asia/Oceania Zones—on the very slow clay of Santiago.

Of course Chile won. That was always to be expected; in fact, Pakistan didn't win a single set. But in this case that was hardly relevant. Fielding Aqeel Khan, a second-singles player ranked 988, against Chile's Fernando Gonzalez at 17, was never going to create a competitive encounter. Indeed the biggest roar from the six thousand spectators in the National Stadium, the spiritual home of Chilean tennis, came when Khan broke Gonzalez's serve in the sixteenth game of the match to claim his first and only game.

At least Qureshi, ranked 355 in singles, made it competitive for a set against Nicolas Massu. Making some judicious approaches to the net, he forced the second set into a tiebreak, but once Massu had taken it 7–4, the match was effectively over.

Qureshi had hoped to show off his best skills in the doubles, where he's ranked 148 and has been as high as 89. But his 12–2 record in Davis Cup doubles was against vastly inferior opposition to the reigning Olympic doubles champions, and he and Khan won just four games as Gonzalez and Massu wrapped up the tie in the shortest possible time.

For Chile it was still a proud weekend, despite the lack of competition. For the first time, the team was captained by Hans Gildemeister, Chile's top player of the 1970s and '80s, whom Gonzalez and Massu admired as children. And they played in their national tennis center, which always inspires great performances from Chileans. But most of the talk centred on who Chile might get in the 2006 World Group, and four days later the balls came out of the hat and handed it a home tie against the Slovak Republic.

As for Pakistan, "I did my best, and I hope my country is proud of me," said Qureshi after losing to Massu. Not only can his country be proud of him, but it can look forward to the day when Qureshi's efforts leave Pakistan with more players to carry the national tennis burden than just one pioneer. ●

Pictured from top:

Aisam Qureshi (PAK) (left) and Nicolas Massu (CHI);

Qureshi battled hard but was no match for the Chileans;

the Chileans celebrated a second year in the elite World Group

SEE AND BE SEEN

Davis Cup by BNP Paribas always attracts the great and good, from the tennis world and beyond, who all come to be a part of the action.

Pictured clockwise from top left: Boris Becker; Boris Yeltsin; Yevgeny Kafelnikov; Kim Clijsters; Rulon Gardner (center), US Gold Medallist in Greco-Roman wrestling at the Athens Olympics; Maria Sharapova (in hood); Ex-Croatian Prime Minister Zlatko Matesa (left) and Croatian Tennis Association President Radimir Cacic (right); Kevin Costner; Gavin Rossdale (left), former lead singer of Bush, and former player Murphy Jensen; Kathi Wenusch (left), girlfriend of Thomas Muster, and (right) Steffi Graf, athletics silver medallist for Austria at the Sydney Olympics

Name

RAFAEL NADAL

Born

JUNE 3, 1986,
IN MALLORCA, SPAIN

Turned professional

2001

Rafael Nadal put himself on the line on all three days in Spain's Play-off tie against Italy, winning both his singles and losing a tense five-set doubles rubber alongside Feliciano Lopez. Visitors to www.daviscup.com recognized his commitment to Spain's cause by voting him their player of the Play-offs.

PLAYER OF THE ROUND

IT WAS A QUIRK of timing that robbed the 2005 Davis Cup by BNP Paribas of a leading role for Rafael Nadal. But in the year the Mallorcan teenager took the tennis world by storm, he did write a significant postscript in the team competition he has come to love.

It's hard to believe that, by the first weekend of March, Nadal still had a fair bit to prove. He had won two tournaments on the clay of Latin America, but the opinion Andy Roddick offered at the 2004 Davis Cup final—that this was a potentially great player who still had to show he could win consistently rather than win just a few big matches—still counted as valid. His late arrival in Bratislava for Spain's first-round tie against the Slovak Republic meant he was rested on the opening day.

It seemed a sensible decision at the time, especially with Feliciano Lopez and Fernando Verdasco able to play singles on a fast court after Nadal had been playing on clay on a different continent. But based on hindsight, it was an appalling error. Not only did both Lopez and Verdasco lose, and with their defeats went Spain's chances of defending their title, but Nadal then embarked on one of the most outstanding runs in world tennis—and not just on clay.

So by the time Spain came to the tricky task of staying in the World Group with an away Play-off tie against Italy, Nadal was not only keen to volunteer, but to volunteer for duty on all three days, even though he had another late arrival—this time from Beijing, where he had won his tenth title of the year five days earlier.

"The Davis Cup is one of my priorities," he explained. "I love to play for my country and I love the team competitions." But did he really know what he was getting himself into?

First he had to pick up the pieces after Juan Carlos Ferrero's shock five-sets defeat to Andreas Seppi. Italy was unlucky not to have their top player, Filippo Volandri, available, but even Volandri would probably have done little better against Nadal than his compatriot Daniele Bracciali did in the second rubber, which Nadal won in straight sets. Then came the doubles, Spain's perennial Achilles heel. In 2004 Nadal formed a useful team with Tommy Robredo. This time it was his friend Lopez by his side, but the worst result possible—defeat, and a long defeat—was the outcome. By Saturday night Nadal was tired.

But this was not just an energetic teenager. This was the indefatigable Rafael Nadal, fighter par excellence, and fight he did. The Spanish journalist Neus Yerro said in early 2004: "This kid is so competitive. Once he has won one Davis Cup, he'll want to win another, and then another, until he can't play anymore. He's that kind of person." And Nadal did want another. After an exhausting year, which had seen him rise from 51 to 2 in the rankings, he was still willing to give everything for Spain to have a chance of a third Davis Cup title in 2006. He looked vulnerable when Seppi won the third set of their fourth rubber 7–5, but Nadal ground his way through the southern Italian heat to level the tie, and set up Ferrero's relatively easy fifth-rubber win.

"I've had a tough week or so with the China Open, the flight back from China, and then a singles on Friday and a doubles on Saturday that lasted for four and a half hours," he said after beating Seppi. "But I played with my heart right until the end. It was my faith in victory when it became tough physically that was the key." ●

the final 2–4 DECEMBER

Croatia defeated Slovak Republic 3–2   BRATISLAVA, SLOVAK REPUBLIC—INDOOR HARD

THE FINAL
SLOVAK REPUBLIC
v **CROATIA**

"QUALITY, NOT QUANTITY" COULD have been the motto for the 2005 Final of the Davis Cup by BNP Paribas.

The Slovak Republic's National Tennis Center had been built with Davis Cup ties in mind, but was the 4,100-seater Sibamac Arena big enough to host a final? And if not, what were the alternatives? Would the world be interested in a final involving two lesser-known nations? And with the Slovaks' second player, Karol Beck, ultimately proving unavailable, would the disparity in strength of the two sides wreck this Final as a spectacle?

In all respects it came up trumps. The ITF sanctioned the Slovak Tennis Association's decision to opt for the National Tennis Center in preference to the neighboring ice hockey arena (which would have offered a couple of thousand more seats but at great cost and in an aging building). And while the crowd capacity will go down as one of the smaller ones for a Davis Cup by BNP Paribas Final, the building proved a worthy venue for the biggest occasion in team tennis. A few days after suggesting a play-off match between Sasa Tuksar and Goran Ivanisevic (see page 78), Croatia's captain, Niki Pilic, scrapped the idea and announced that if Ivanisevic was fit, he would be Croatia's fourth player. Ivanisevic promptly embarked on a two-month practice regime that got him into better shape than at the end of his playing days, and his involvement helped raise the profile of the Final in the weeks leading up to it. And far from being one-sided, the Final went to a live fifth rubber with some new records set, providing a glorious culmination of the 2005 tennis year.

If the Final offered an opportunity for tennis to establish deeper roots in the Slovak Republic alongside the country's premier sporting passions of football and ice hockey, it was also an opportunity for the nation to increase its profile in the global sporting consciousness.

The Slovaks gained independence from the Austro-Hungarian Empire at the end of World War II, when they teamed up with the Czechs to form Czechoslovakia. The partnership lasted until their amicable divorce at the end of 1992 when both became independent, sovereign states. The Slovaks, a very religious people, are proud of their culture of hard work. Rogue traders in the streets of the historic center of Bratislava could be found selling Hard Rock Café T-shirts doctored to read "Hard Work Café," and one taxi driver boasted proudly: "Do you know who built Prague? We did. The Czechs had the brains, and the Slovaks the hard work, so they designed it and we built it."

Bratislava was also a timely location for the 2005 Final. In December 1805, the city—then known by its German name, Pressburg—was host to a peace conference that marked the height of Napoléon Bonaparte's powers. The French ruler's crushing victory over the armies of the Holy Roman Emperor Franz II at the battle of Austerlitz led France to claim several Austrian territories. So in December 2005 the city's traditional Christmas craft market was augmented by celebrations of the two hundredth anniversary of the Treaty of

Pictured previous page:
The Croatian team celebrates an historic first
Davis Cup by BNP Paribas title
Pictured top to bottom:
The Sibamac Arena National Tennis Center was small but
very well-appointed, and provided a great venue for the Final;
Goran Ivanisevic (CRO) and Miloslav Mecir (Captain, SVK)
received the ITF/ITHF Davis Cup Award of Excellence;
the Christmas market in Bratislava

Pressburg. And on December 2, the two hundredth anniversary of Napoléon's victory at Austerlitz, the eyes and ears of the tennis world fell on Bratislava as the first Davis Cup Final in thirty years to feature two nations never to have won the trophy got underway.

France's official representative at the Final, Sandra de Jenken, was making her own piece of history, though a more benign one than her military compatriot. The thirty-one-year-old from Nice became the first woman to umpire a match in the Davis Cup by BNP Paribas Final, when she took charge of the opener between Ivan Ljubicic and Karol Kucera. Not only did she handle the match with admirable invisibility, but Ljubicic paid an unprompted compliment to all the officials in his post-match news conference.

"They were really unbelievable today," he said. "It's really nice to see that even when you play away, with all the linesmen from the Slovak Republic, they didn't make one single mistake." You can't quite imagine John McEnroe saying that.

By then, Ljubicic had made his own piece of history—at McEnroe's expense. His 6–3 6–4 6–3 victory over Karol Kucera made him the first player to win ten live rubbers in one year since the Davis Cup format was changed twenty-five years earlier to the four-ties-per-year World Group structure. The rubber also proved a milestone for Kucera: his last match at tour level before retirement.

It was a nice touch that Kucera, the man who first put the Slovak Republic on the map as a tennis nation after the break-up of Czechoslovakia, could play an active part in the greatest moment in Slovak tennis history, though he might have wished for a happier chain of circumstances leading to his participation. The Slovak team that reached the Final had Dominik Hrbaty as its linchpin, with Karol Beck playing second singles and teaming up with Michal Mertinak in the doubles. But Beck hadn't played for several weeks leading up to the Final, and withdrew from the Bratislava Challenger tournament two weeks before, citing knee problems. He hardly practiced at all with his teammates in the week of the Final, while Kucera was a regular hitting partner of Hrbaty. The word was that Beck's knee was still causing concern, though Slovak journalists probed hard—in vain—for confirmation of more sinister rumors about Beck's absence. When Beck was nominated for singles and the doubles at the draw ceremony, normal service appeared to have resumed.

Yet at 11 o'clock on the Friday morning, the Slovak Republic requested a change of player. Once first-day nominations have been made, Davis Cup by BNP Paribas rules stipulate that changes can only be made with a certificate from an independent doctor and approval from the referee. Such approval was given, and Kucera was in for Beck. The ten games he won against the Davis Cup's Player of the Year proved a creditable end to a loyal career, but in truth Ljubicic was never behind and never seriously threatened. He had earned his record tenth live win in a single year—beating John McEnroe's previous mark of nine from 1982—with one of his easiest matches, a far cry from the hoops he jumped through to beat Andre Agassi, Andy Roddick, and Nikolay Davydenko, all Top-Tenners.

Ljubicic's win made the second singles a must-win for the hosts. But if that put pressure on Dominik Hrbaty, it hardly showed. "Of course I feel pressure like any other player would," the twenty-seven-year-old Bratislavan had said after the draw, "but I will enjoy the match and enjoy the time being there. If I win I win, if I lose I lose, I'll do my best, that's all I can do. If I win I'll be happy, if I lose it's only sport."

Pictured top to bottom:

Sandra de Jenken (center) was the first female official to umpire in a Davis Cup by BNP Paribas Final; Miloslav Mecir (Captain, SVK)

Perhaps that philosophical attitude allowed Hrbaty to play one of his best matches. The opening set had little to choose between the players. The Slovak was more confident from the baseline, but Ancic earned numerous cheap points from his cleverly varied serve. They went to the tiebreak, but once Hrbaty had taken it, the ways began to part. Hrbaty grew in confidence, the angst that caused Ancic to lose all his first-day singles rubbers in 2005 reared its head again, and two breaks saw the Slovak take a two-sets lead. Ancic could have knocked Hrbaty off course when he won the third-set tiebreak, but at the very time the twenty-one-year-old Croat needed to pile on the pressure, it was Hrbaty who rediscovered his best form and rode out a 7–6(4) 6–3 6–7(4) 6–4 winner. When asked after the match when he had last served that well, Hrbaty chuckled and said: "When I was about eight years old."

Having beaten John McEnroe's record for live rubbers in a World Group year, Ljubicic then went on to make it eleven in his and Ancic's fourth doubles win of the year. The Olympic bronze medalists, who had never lost a Davis Cup rubber, beat Dominik Hrbaty and Michal Mertinak 7–6(5) 6–3 7–6(5) in an absorbing match that made up in tension what it sometimes lacked in quality.

Croatia were clear favorites from the moment it was confirmed that Beck would not be able to partner Mertinak. Like Ancic and Ljubicic, Beck and Mertinak were unbeaten in Davis Cup doubles coming into the Final but would have started as slight underdogs against the more powerful visitors. With Beck out, it would have been a shock if Croatia had lost, but with Hrbaty on a high from beating Ancic, there was always a hope for the home side that he could bring his talismanic qualities to the Slovak pairing.

It didn't happen. Hrbaty was arguably the weakest of the four—he bounced around and constantly geed up his more languid partner, but a handful of missed volleys proved costly, especially in the first set when the Slovaks were the better pair. Twice they broke—they even served for the set at 5–4—but twice they were broken back in the next game. When Croatia took the first set on a Ljubicic ace, the home pair had nothing to show for their dominance, and that put the wind into Croatia's sails. Ljubicic said later he felt the tennis he and Ancic delivered in the second set was the best doubles they had played all year.

The home pair's best chance to get back into the match came in the seventh game of the third set. With Ancic serving at 3–3 and looking the more vulnerable of the two Croats, the Slovak Republic had two break points. Ancic saved them with some big serving, and that proved crucial, not just for the doubles but for the destiny of the Davis Cup. After that he grew in confidence, and while the second tiebreak was as tight as the first, the visitors were always ahead and posted a 2–1 lead in two hours, forty-nine minutes.

Thus far the Final had followed exactly the pattern of Croatia's three previous ties in 2005: first day's singles split, followed by a win in the doubles. For the pattern to continue Ivan Ljubicic would need to equal another of John McEnroe's records—twelve wins in twelve matches, posted in 1982—and seal the trophy for Croatia. But while that would have had a certain symmetry about it, it would have made Croatia's triumph seem very much a Ljubicic achievement, with Ancic as little more than his doubles partner. In a dramatic final day, the pattern was to be broken, and Ancic was to have his moment.

THE FINAL

Pictured opposite top to bottom:

Karol Kucera (SVK), a father-figure to Slovak tennis, was no match for Ivan Ljubicic in the opening singles. It proved to be the last match of Kucera's illustrious career; Ivan Ljubicic (CRO) made it ten wins from ten live rubbers by defeating Kucera, a new record

Pictured top to bottom:

Mario Ancic (left) and Ivan Ljubicic (CRO) won all four doubles rubbers they played in Davis Cup in 2005; Michal Mertinak (left) and Dominik Hrbaty (SVK) found Ancic/Ljubicic too hot to handle in the doubles

Unbeknown to the Slovak and Croatian fans in the Sibamac Arena on the final day of the 2005 tennis year, Ljubicic had woken up with a badly cricked neck. He spent much of the morning being massaged and manipulated, and taking medication to ease the muscles.

"It has happened before," he explained later, "I think it's caused by all the different hotel rooms we stay in—some are air conditioned, and the pillows can be different." With Goran Ivanisevic not trusting himself over the best of five sets, having played only on the seniors tour, Ivo Karlovic stood by to take Ljubicic's place. At five minutes to one, with the deadline for changes to nominations looming, Croatia's captain, Niki Pilic, left the decision to Ljubicic. Ljubicic said he would give it a go, and an hour later the two players walked on court as if nothing had happened.

The result was the best match of the Final. Perhaps because he couldn't serve as well as normal due to the pain involved in lifting his head, Ljubicic got involved in more rallies. He sliced more than usual on his backhand and chipped back several forehands, all to keep from giving Hrbaty a regular rhythm. For his part, Hrbaty worked the angles well, peppering the Ljubicic backhand, pushing him further out of court, and then attacking to the Ljubicic forehand that at times proved very inconsistent. There were too many errors for it to be a frontline classic, but with the Davis Cup so close—and in both players' line of vision whenever they walked to their chairs—the level of play was remarkably high given the nerves involved.

Ljubicic took the first set thanks to an early break, but when Hrbaty broke in the second game of the second set, the tide turned the home side's way. Ljubicic went into something of a slump, and when he served four double faults in successive service games early in the third set to give Hrbaty a double break, it looked most likely to be a four-sets victory for the home favorite. At one stage Ljubicic took a bathroom break and was sick, the medication for his neck muscles having upset his stomach. He looked dead on his feet as the match wore on, but his big serve kept him in it. Then Hrbaty threw in a bad game midway through the fourth set, and suddenly it was 2–2.

Hrbaty had the advantage of serving first in the decider, and that proved crucial at 5–4 when he connected with some returns to set up match point. Ljubicic saved the first with a glorious down-the-line backhand, and he saved the second with a big serve, but on the third, Hrbaty challenged his opponent to hit another backhand winner, Ljubicic netted, and three thousand fans wildly celebrated the home player's 4–6 6–3 6–4 3–6 6–4 win in three hours, twenty minutes.

Was it Hrbaty's best-ever match? "Maybe I've played better matches than this one," he said courtside as he got his breath back, "but with the atmosphere and the pressure and everything around, it was one of my toughest matches and I'm so glad I won."

Hrbaty refused to look at the Davis Cup, for he knew it was still a long way from being won—his heroics had merely given the Slovak Republic the chance of a shock upset. For Beck's absence was to be felt powerfully in the fifth rubber. Faced with the choice of Karol Kucera, the experienced father figure of Slovak tennis but with a ranking down at 297, or the 165th-ranked Michal Mertinak, a twenty-six-year-old whose tennis had been played mostly on the Challenger circuit, the Slovak Republic's captain, Milos Mecir, opted for Mertinak, whose showing in the doubles had been impressive.

Pictured top to bottom:
Ljubicic was finally floored in the 2005 Davis Cup by an inspired Dominik Hrbaty; Hrbaty showed passion and commitment in abundance all weekend, along with some exceptional play; nobody could doubt what representing his country meant to Hrbaty

Pictured opposite top to bottom:
Hrbaty receives the congratulations of the Slovak bench; Mario Ancic (CRO) finally won a live singles rubber in 2005 for Croatia—and what a one to win!

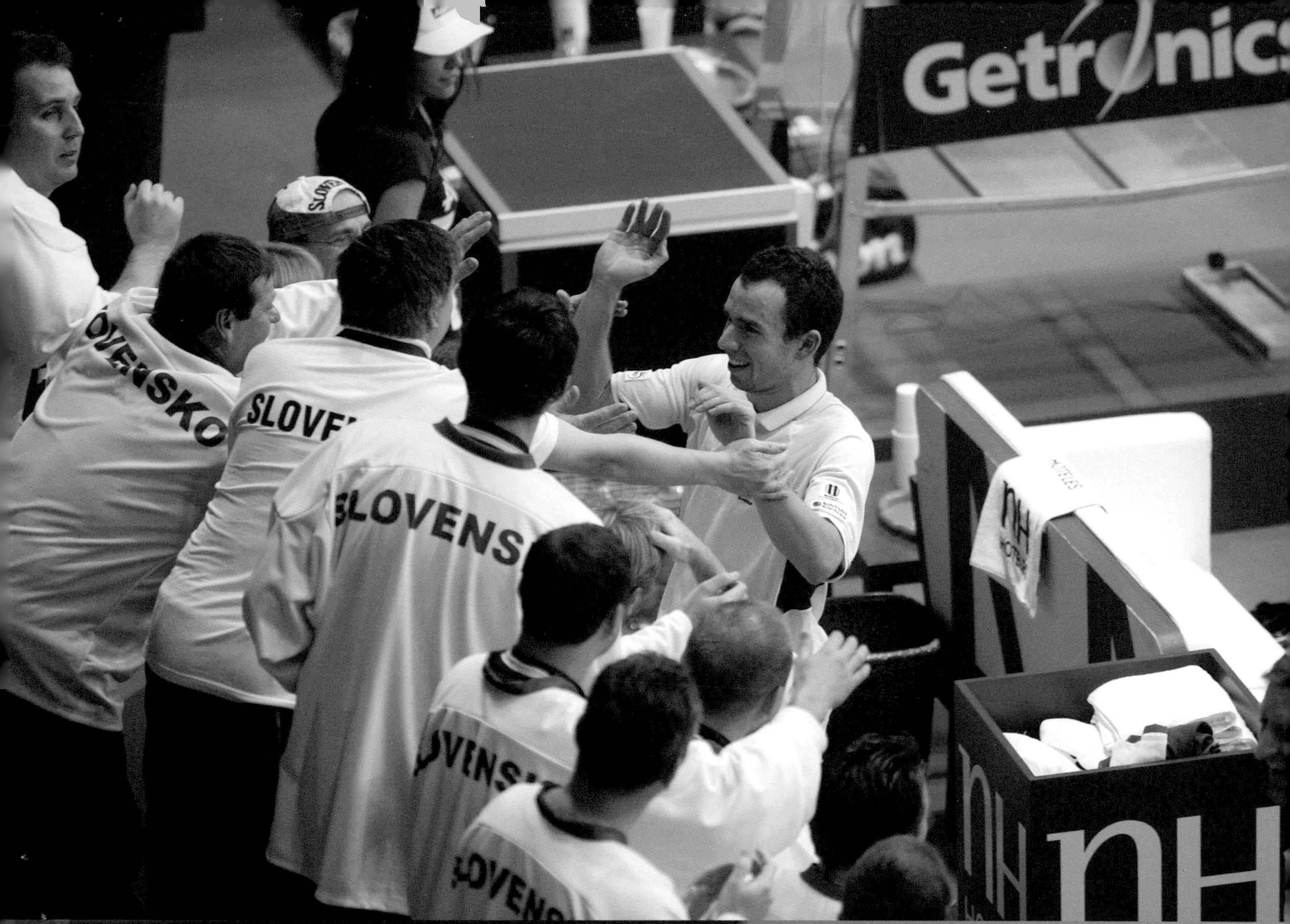
Getronics

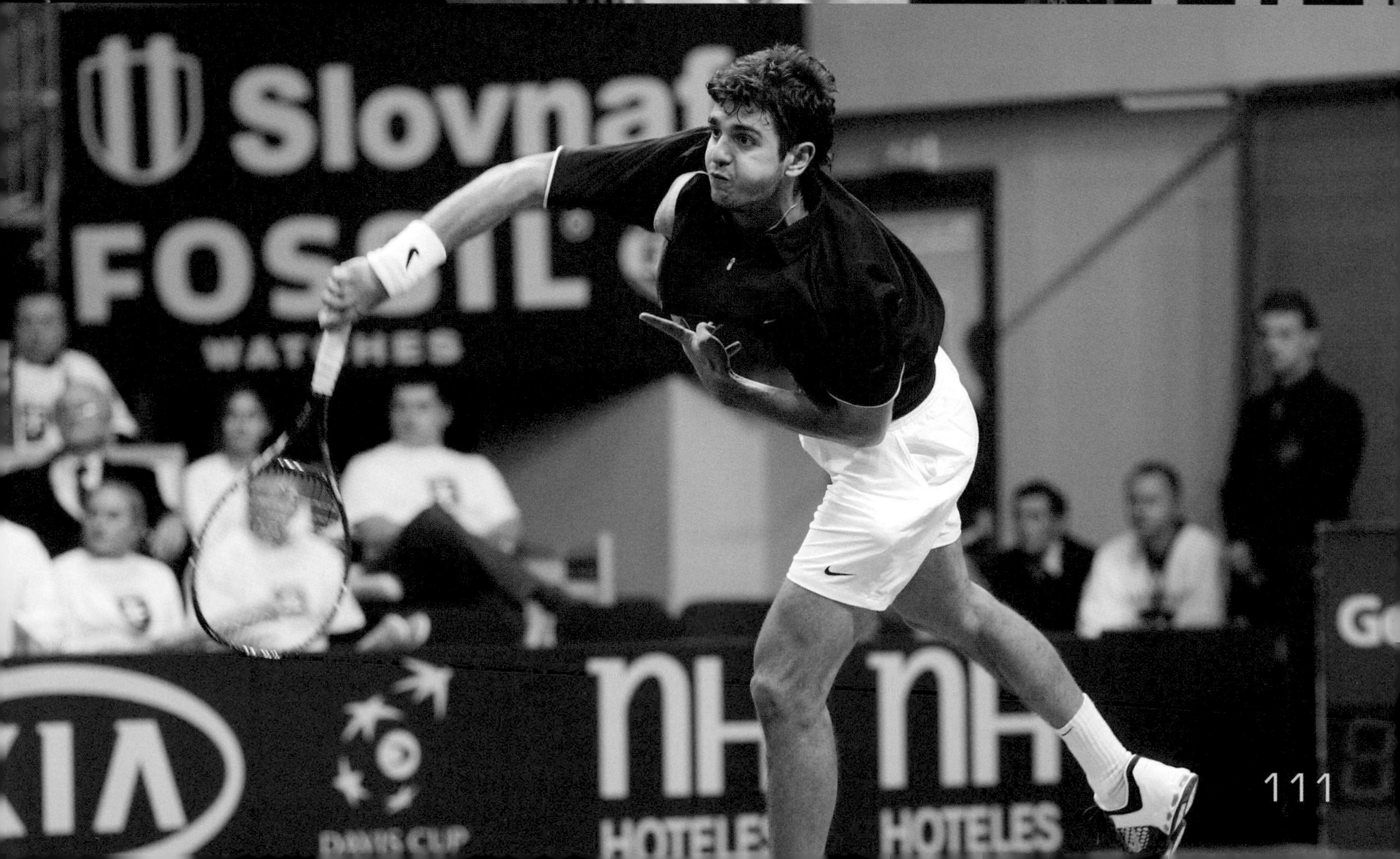
FOSSIL
WATCHES
nH
HOTELES
nH
HOTELES
DAVIS CUP

Pictured top to bottom:

Both the Slovak fans (top) and Croatian fans (center) provided
a colorful, noisy backdrop to the Final; Michal Mertinak (SVK)
played well above his ranking in the final deciding rubber

Pictured opposite top to bottom:

Mario Ancic (left) and Ivan Ljubicic, Croatia's Davis Cup heroes;
the 2005 Davis Cup by BNP Paribas Champion Nation—Croatia
(left to right: Ivo Karlovic, Goran Ivanisevic, Captain Niki Pilic,
Mario Ancic and Ivan Ljubicic)

Nor was it entirely clear whom Croatia would choose. Mario Ancic had yet to win a live singles rubber all year so was a slightly risky choice. Yet his ranking was 22, so it would have been a bold gamble to replace him with Ivo Karlovic at 72 or the sentimental choice, the ranking-less Goran Ivanisevic. In the end it was Ancic v Mertinak. Mertinak fully justified his selection with a plucky display that impressed many, but the climax was to prove the making of Mario Ancic.

Slightly surprised by the quality of the opposition he was facing, Ancic wisely opted to play a controlled first set. He had several break points on the Mertinak serve, but the Slovak saved them all with some bold net play. Yet when it came to the tiebreak, Ancic played his best tennis, Mertinak showed his limitations, and Croatia had the first set. With a break in the second game of the second set, Ancic was cruising to victory, and when he broke at the start of the third, it looked all over for the home side.

But Mertinak then broke back for 3–3 and held for 4–3. Was a fightback on the cards? Ancic leveled at 4–4. Then Mertinak made a couple of errors—understandable ones as his only chance was to play a high-risk strategy of coming at Ancic at every reasonable opportunity—and suddenly it was Croatia serving for the Cup. Three superb points saw Ancic race to 40–0. He chipped a sliced approach shot long on the first match point, but on the eighth stroke of the second, a Mertinak forehand went just long, and the Croatians were the champions on a 7–6(1) 6–3 6–4 scoreline.

As Ancic punched the air and tore off his shirt, the first man out to hug him was Ljubicic. He had said before the Final that it didn't matter whether he broke any individual records or not—what mattered to him was that Croatia won the Cup. It had finally done so, and Ljubicic was going to be first out there, even at the risk of having to retreat rapidly if Mertinak's shot had been on the baseline instead of just over it! But there was no doubt, the celebrations began, and Ancic had finally contributed his singles share to what, at the final hurdle, had become a true team effort.

Because the stadium was relatively small, Croatia received a larger than normal percentage of the tickets, and it became a sea of the distinctive red-and-white check of Croatia. The passion with which the Croatian fans sang their national anthem at the trophy presentation ceremony sent shivers down the spines of nearly everyone in the arena, and left no doubt that this was a victory that meant something massive—certainly on a par with Croatia's two previous sporting highlights: reaching the semifinals of the 1998 soccer World Cup and Ivanisevic's Wimbledon triumph in 2001. The next morning thousands of supporters turned up in Zagreb, Croatia's capital, to welcome the team home.

"It's a dream for such a small country to win this competition," said Ancic. "It's remarkable, it showed a lot of team spirit. We will always cherish it."

And Ljubicic, his voice breaking with emotion just as it had after the Semifinals, added: "I wanted this so hard, because my career is great but without any big titles, and finally I have this one."

Clutching his trophy replica like a newborn baby, Ljubicic said: "I have to build something special for this, it's really beautiful, aesthetically it's fantastic."

If in some people's eyes it was an unfashionable final, it had delivered a great spectacle. Even the Slovaks left the arena with every reason to feel not just pride in the

Pictured top to bottom:
Thousands of fans gave the Croatian team
a heroes' welcome in Zagreb; Ancic and Ljubicic
with the Davis Cup trophy
Pictured opposite:
For Ancic and Ljubicic, it was a dream end to a
year they will never forget

SLOVAK REPUBLIC v **CROATIA** CONTINUED

achievements of their team but a sense of participation in an event that may well not happen again in the small central European nation for another generation. And four hours later the Slovak players were smiling, singing, and cheering as the post-final official dinner featured a marvelous celebration of Slovak musical culture that had everyone present feeling they had been part of something special.

It was the first final for four years to feature live radio-style commentary on the official Davis Cup website, www.daviscup.com. A feature of the Davis Cup Radio presented by Getronics broadcast was the number of Slovak and Croatian expatriates who e-mailed questions and messages of appreciation from around the globe. One Croatian couple who had lived in America for twenty-five years and didn't have access to television coverage from Bratislava wrote: "Your coverage of this Final means more to us than you will ever know." Such were the passions this Final engendered from the citizens of two nations that had never scaled such heights before.

It was also a final of historical milestones: the first woman to umpire a final, the first player to win eleven live rubbers in a World Group year, and Niki Pilic becoming the first captain to win the Davis Cup with two nations. In 1988 and 1989 he won it with West Germany, and in 1993 he won it with a united Germany, but winning it in 2005 with the country of his birth (even if it wasn't a sovereign state when he was born) meant just a little bit more to him. "I was very high when I won with Germany," he had said before the Final, "but if I win it with Croatia it'll be like being on Mount Everest."

The Final highlighted the global expansion of tennis. It sent the message to the established Davis Cup nations that new members are joining the club of top teams. Croatia was only the twelfth country to add its name to the roll of honor in the competition's 105-year history, but both its success and that of the Slovak Republic suggest there will be more new names in coming years.

And it brought the Croatian team that took Yugoslavia to the 1991 Semifinals full circle. Though he didn't play in the Final and was very mindful of not detracting from Ljubicic's and Ancic's credit, the 2005 Davis Cup by BNP Paribas Final was also a triumph for Goran Ivanisevic. As a member of the nominated foursome, he received the medal and trophy replica he had worked so hard for and must have given up hope of ever winning. With Ivanisevic ending his top-level playing career by picking up the biggest and most coveted prize in team tennis, the 2005 tennis year ended with both drama and a sense of natural sporting justice. ●

OUTSIDE THE LINES

While all the attention is normally focused on what happens on court, a big part of the Davis Cup by BNP Paribas is what happens off court at ties. Dinners, draws, interviews, parties—they all bring a unique sense of team-spirit and enjoyment to the world of tennis.

Name
IVAN LJUBICIC

Born
MARCH 19, 1979
IN BANJA LUKA,
BOSNIA & HERZEGOVINA

Turned professional
1998

There is no question Ivan Ljubicic was the 2005 Player of the Davis Cup by BNP Paribas. He won eleven live rubbers, a record for the World Group, and despite losing his last match—a glorious five-setter against Dominik Hrbaty—he was still voted the player of the Final by visitors to the competition's official website, www.daviscup.com.

PLAYER OF THE YEAR

IF THERE WAS A point at which Ivan Ljubicic's glorious year in 2005 could be said to have started, it was probably in November 2003 when he began working with the Spanish fitness coach, Salvador Sosa. Ljubicic recalls: "He told me when we started 'the first year's going to be good, but the second year will be the best,' and he was right."

As well as being the Davis Cup by BNP Paribas Player of the Year, Ljubicic has the right to be considered the indoor player of 2005. He won the ATP titles in Metz and Vienna, he reached six other finals, five of them indoors, and he pushed Roger Federer and Rafael Nadal the full distance in three of them. He thanks the Davis Cup for reviving his tour fortunes after the US Open, when his brilliant start to the year (four finals in eight weeks) seemed a distant memory. "I was focusing just on Davis Cup after the Semifinal against Russia," he says, "not really thinking much about the tour, and perhaps that helped me with my great run and qualification for the Tennis Masters Cup?"

Any player who dominates the Davis Cup by BNP Paribas is going to be fiercely patriotic, and Ljubicic is no exception. But above all the other players who have dominated the competition in recent years, Ljubicic is much more a citizen of the world. After his Croatian parents helped him escape from the horrors of the Yugoslav civil war and take refuge in Italy, he could have had one of three nationalities: Bosnian, Italian, or Croatian (he even enquired about Italian citizenship at one point).

That has given him a refreshingly polyglot perspective on his success for Croatia. Asked if Bosnia and Italy have a share in his 2005 success, he replied: "I think they do. I was born in Bosnia and lived there for the first twelve years of my life. I moved to Italy in 1993, I've spent a lot of time in Italy, most of the people around me are Italian, so it's very difficult for me to say 'I'm Croatian and who cares about the others.' I feel pretty international, but I'm glad we did it for Croatia, because that's the country that gave me the most, the biggest things."

It's easy to look at the drama of Ljubicic's childhood and put his success on court down to those struggles. Does Ljubicic himself?

"Not directly. You never think about those things on the court, but in life it probably helps because you're tougher, you're stronger, you have to succeed, otherwise you're not going to survive. Especially in the beginning of your career, it helps, it drives you through because you have no choice. It's always a problem if you have a choice: you can go to school, you have a car, so why should you play? But I had nothing so I was forced to succeed. It's not only that; of course, I always wanted to be as good as I could be as well."

So what will he be telling his children and grandchildren about his glorious year in 2005?

"I hope it's not the best! I do feel good. That victory in Carson was historic, and I'm glad that we finished by winning the title—it would be very easily forgotten if we lost in the second round or the Semifinal. But I hope the best is still to come." ●

WORLD GROUP

First Round 4-6 March

Slovak Republic defeated Spain 4-1, Bratislava, SVK; Hard (I): Karol Beck (SVK) d. Feliciano Lopez (ESP) 64 75 63; Dominik Hrbaty (SVK) d. Fernando Verdasco (ESP) 63 64 67(7) 63; Karol Beck/Michal Mertinak (SVK) d. Albert Costa/Rafael Nadal (ESP) 76(3) 64 76(8); Michal Mertinak (SVK) d. Feliciano Lopez (ESP) 60 67(3) 64; Fernando Verdasco (ESP) d. Kamil Capkovic (SVK) 62 62.

Netherlands defeated Switzerland 3-2, Fribourg, SUI; Hard (I): Sjeng Schalken (NED) d. Marco Chiudinelli (SUI) 76(4) 46 63 57 62; Peter Wessels (NED) d. Stanislas Wawrinka (SUI) 76(12) 67(4) 76(7) 64; Yves Allegro/George Bastl (SUI) d. Dennis Van Scheppingen/Peter Wessels (NED) 57 46 76(5) 75 97; Sjeng Schalken (NED) d. Stanislas Wawrinka (SUI) 16 62 64 26 97; Marco Chiudinelli (SUI) d. Peter Wessels (NED) 46 ret.

Australia defeated Austria 5-0, Sydney, AUS; Grass (O): Lleyton Hewitt (AUS) d. Alexander Peya (AUT) 62 63 64; Wayne Arthurs (AUS) d. Jurgen Melzer (AUT) 76(5) 62 64; Wayne Arthurs/Todd Woodbridge (AUS) d. Julian Knowle/Jurgen Melzer (AUT) 46 63 26 64 75; Todd Woodbridge (AUS) d. Marco Mirnegg (AUT) 63 46 75; Chris Guccione (AUS) d. Alexander Peya (AUT) 63 64.

Argentina defeated Czech Republic 5-0 Buenos Aires, ARG; Clay (O): David Nalbandian (ARG) d. Jiri Novak (CZE) 46 62 63 64; Guillermo Coria (ARG) d. Tomas Berdych (CZE) 63 36 60 63; Guillermo Canas/David Nalbandian (ARG) d. Jan Hernych/Tomas Zib (CZE) 63 46 61 62; Guillermo Coria (ARG) d. Jan Hernych (CZE) 63 60; Agustin Calleri (ARG) d. Tomas Zib (CZE) 62 64.

Russia defeated Chile 4-1, Moscow, RUS; Carpet (I): Fernando Gonzalez (CHI) d. Mikhail Youzhny (RUS) 76(4) 57 63 76(4); Marat Safin (RUS) d. Adrian Garcia (CHI) 61 36 63 76(4); Marat Safin/Mikhail Youzhny (RUS) d. Adrian Garcia/Fernando Gonzalez (CHI) 63 64 63; Marat Safin (RUS) d. Fernando Gonzalez (CHI) 76(4) 76(5) 16 67(3) 64; Nikolay Davydenko (RUS) d. Paul Capdeville (CHI) 62 61.

France defeated Sweden 3-2, Strasbourg, FRA; Clay (I): Paul-Henri Mathieu (FRA) d. Joachim Johansson (SWE) 63 64 62; Thomas Johansson (SWE) d. Sebastien Grosjean (FRA) 64 64 76(1); Arnaud Clement/Michael Llodra (FRA) d. Simon Aspelin/Jonas Bjorkman (SWE) 76(5) 64 67(4) 64; Joachim Johansson (SWE) d. Sebastien Grosjean (FRA) 36 61 64 61; Paul-Henri Mathieu (FRA) d. Thomas Johansson (SWE) 61 64 67(4) 64.

Romania defeated Belarus 3-2, Brasov, ROM Clay (I): Max Mirnyi (BLR) d. Victor Hanescu (ROM) 76(6) 64 36 64; Andrei Pavel (ROM) d. Vladimir Voltchkov (BLR) 64 76(2) 76(2); Max Mirnyi/Vladimir Voltchkov (BLR) d. Andrei Pavel/Gabriel Trifu (ROM) 76(3) 63 64; Andrei Pavel (ROM) d. Max Mirnyi (BLR) 61 76(0) 46 63; Victor Hanescu (ROM) d. Vladimir Voltchkov (BLR) 76(2) 64 76(6).

Croatia defeated USA 3-2, Carson, CA, USA; Hard (O): Ivan Ljubicic (CRO) d. Andre Agassi (USA) 63 76(0) 63; Andy Roddick (USA) d. Mario Ancic (CRO) 46 62 61 64; Mario Ancic/Ivan Ljubicic (CRO) d. Bob Bryan/Mike Bryan (USA) 36 76(8) 64 64; Ivan Ljubicic (CRO) d. Andy Roddick (USA) 46 63 76(11) 67(7) 62; Bob Bryan (USA) d. Roko Karanusic (CRO) 62 36 61.

Quarterfinals 15-17 July

Slovak Republic defeated Netherlands 4-1 Bratislava, SVK; Hard (I): Dominik Hrbaty (SVK) d. Raemon Sluiter (NED) 61 57 64 63; Peter Wessels (NED) d. Karol Beck (SVK) 67(5) 75 67(3) 64 62; Karol Beck/Michal Mertinak (SVK) d. Paul Haarhuis/Melle Van Gemerden (NED) 57 63 64 75; Dominik Hrbaty (SVK) d. Peter Wessels (NED) 63 61 30 ret.; Michal Mertinak (SVK) d. Melle Van Gemerden (NED) 46 63 64.

Argentina defeated Australia 4-1, Sydney, AUS; Grass (O): Lleyton Hewitt (AUS) d. Guillermo Coria (ARG) 76(5) 61 16 62; David Nalbandian (ARG) d. Wayne Arthurs (AUS) 63 76(8) 57 62; David Nalbandian/Mariano Puerta (ARG) d. Wayne Arthurs/Lleyton Hewitt (AUS) 76(6) 64 63; David Nalbandian (ARG) d. Lleyton Hewitt (AUS) 62 64 64; Guillermo Coria (ARG) d. Peter Luczak (AUS) 63 76(11).

Russia defeated France 3-2, Moscow, RUS; Clay (I): Richard Gasquet (FRA) d. Igor Andreev (RUS) 64 63 76(1); Nikolay Davydenko (RUS) d. Paul-Henri Mathieu (FRA) 75 62 75; Arnaud Clement/Michael Llodra (FRA) d. Igor Andreev/Mikhail Youzhny (RUS) 75 64 67(3) 62; Nikolay Davydenko (RUS) d. Richard Gasquet (FRA) 62 46 62 61; Igor Andreev (RUS) d. Paul-Henri Mathieu (FRA) 60 62 61.

Croatia defeated Romania 4-1, Split, CRO; Carpet (I): Andrei Pavel (ROM) d. Mario Ancic (CRO) 16 64 46 63 64; Ivan Ljubicic (CRO) d. Victor Hanescu (ROM) 63 62 76(3); Mario Ancic/Ivan Ljubicic (CRO) d. Andrei Pavel/Gabriel Trifu (ROM) 57 64 67(9) 64 64; Ivan Ljubicic (CRO) d. Andrei Pavel (ROM) 63 64 63; Mario Ancic (CRO) d. Victor Hanescu (ROM) 76(3) 76(8).

Semifinals 23-25 September

Slovak Republic defeated Argentina 4-1,Bratislava, SVK; Hard (I): Karol Beck (SVK) d. Guillermo Coria (ARG) 75 64 64; David Nalbandian (ARG) d. Dominik Hrbaty (SVK) 36 75 75 63; Karol Beck/Michal Mertinak (SVK) d. David Nalbandian/Mariano Puerta (ARG) 76(5) 75 76(5); Dominik Hrbaty (SVK) d. Guillermo Coria (ARG) 76(2) 62 63; Karol Kucera (SVK) d. Mariano Puerta (ARG) 46 63 21 ret.

Croatia defeated Russia 3-2, Split, CRO; Carpet (I): Nikolay Davydenko (RUS) d. Mario Ancic (CRO) 75 64 57 64;Ivan Ljubicic (CRO) d. Mikhail Youzhny (RUS) 36 63 64 46 64; Mario Ancic/Ivan Ljubicic (CRO) d. Igor Andreev/Dmitry Tursunov (RUS) 62 46 76(5) 36 64; Ivan Ljubicic (CRO) d. Nikolay Davydenko (RUS) 63 76(6) 64; Dmitry Tursunov (RUS) d. Ivo Karlovic (CRO) 64 64.

Final 2-4 December

Croatia defeated Slovak Republic 3-2, Bratislava, SVK; Hard (I): Ivan Ljubicic (CRO) d. Karol Kucera (SVK) 63 64 63; Dominik Hrbaty (SVK) d. Mario Ancic (CRO) 76(4) 63 67(4) 64; Mario Ancic/Ivan Ljubicic (CRO) d. Dominik Hrbaty/Michal Mertinak (SVK) 76(5) 63 76(5); Dominik Hrbaty (SVK) d. Ivan Ljubicic (CRO) 46 63 64 36 64; Mario Ancic (CRO) d. Michal Mertinak (SVK) 76(1) 63 64.

World Group Play-Offs 23-25 September

Austria defeated Ecuador 4-1, Portschach, AUT; Hard (O): Jurgen Melzer (AUT) d. Giovanni Lapentti (ECU) 61 60 62; Nicolas Lapentti (ECU) d. Stefan Koubek (AUT) 57 46 64 76(5) 75; Julian Knowle/Jurgen Melzer (AUT) d. Giovanni Lapentti/Nicolas Lapentti (ECU) 26 64 60 63; Jurgen Melzer (AUT) d. Nicolas Lapentti (ECU) 75 64 75; Stefan Koubek (AUT) d. Carlos Avellan (ECU) 63 62.

Belarus defeated Canada 3-2, Toronto, CAN; Hard (O): Frank Dancevic (CAN) d. Vladimir Voltchkov (BLR) 57 64 46 76(3) 63;Max Mirnyi (BLR) d. Daniel Nestor (CAN) 67(4) 75 21 ret; Daniel Nestor/Frederic Niemeyer (CAN) d. Max Mirnyi/Vladimir Voltchkov (BLR) 75 62 36 76(6); Max Mirnyi (BLR) d. Frank Dancevic (CAN) 46 63 64 36 64; Vladimir Voltchkov (BLR) d. Frederic Niemeyer (CAN) 62 67(2) 63 64.

Chile defeated Pakistan 5-0, Santiago, CHI; Clay (O): Fernando Gonzalez (CHI) d. Aqeel Khan (PAK) 60 60 61; Nicolas Massu (CHI) d. Aisam Qureshi (PAK) 62 76(4) 61; Fernando Gonzalez/Nicolas Massu (CHI) d. Aqeel Khan/Aisam Qureshi (PAK) 61 63 60; Paul Capdeville (CHI) d. Shahzad Khan (PAK) 60 61; Adrian Garcia (CHI) d. Aqeel Khan (PAK) 62 64.

Germany defeated Czech Republic 3-2, Liberec, CZE; Clay (I): Tomas Berdych (CZE) d. Tommy Haas (GER) 46 46 61 76(9) 63; Nicolas Kiefer (GER) d. Tomas Zib (CZE) 760 64 76(5) 60; Tommy Haas/Alexander Waske (GER) d. Frantisek Cermak/Leos Friedl (CZE) 46 75 62 26 64; Tomas Berdych (CZE) d. Nicolas Kiefer (GER) 67(5) 63 26 64 75; Tommy Haas (GER) d. Tomas Zib (CZE) 67(3) 75 62 60.

Spain defeated Italy 3-2, Torre del Greco, ITA; Clay (O): Andreas Seppi (ITA) d. Juan Carlos Ferrero (ESP) 57 36 60 63 62; Rafael Nadal (ESP) d. Daniele Bracciali (ITA) 63 64 61; Daniele Bracciali/Giorgio Galimberti (ITA) d. Feliciano Lopez/Rafael Nadal (ESP) 46 64 62 46 97; Rafael Nadal (ESP) d. Andreas Seppi (ITA) 61 62 57 64; Juan Carlos Ferrero (ESP) d. Daniele Bracciali (ITA) 63 60 63.

Sweden defeated India 3-1, New Delhi, IND; Grass (O): Jonas Bjorkman (SWE) d. Prakash Amritraj (IND) 64 64 64;Thomas Johansson (SWE) d. Rohan Bopanna (IND) 76(3) 76(2) 76(4); Mahesh Bhupathi/Leander Paes (IND) d. Simon Aspelin/Jonas Bjorkman (SWE) 36 63 64 63; Thomas Johansson (SWE) d. Prakash Amritraj (IND) 64 63 62; fifth rubber not played.

Switzerland defeated Great Britain 5-0, Geneva, SUI; Clay (I): Roger Federer (SUI) d. Alan Mackin (GBR) 60 60 62; Stanislas Wawrinka (SUI) d. Andy Murray (GBR) 63 76(5) 64; Yves Allegro/Roger Federer (SUI) d. Andy Murray/Greg Rusedski (GBR) 75 26 76(1) 62; George Bastl (SUI) d. David Sherwood (GBR) 63 60; Stanislas Wawrinka (SUI) d. Alan Mackin (GBR) 75 76(5).

USA defeated Belgium 4-1, Leuven, BEL; Clay (I): Olivier Rochus (BEL) d. James Blake (USA) 64 75 61; Andy Roddick (USA) d. Christophe Rochus (BEL) 61 62 63; Bob Bryan/Mike Bryan (USA) d. Olivier Rochus/Kristof Vliegen (BEL) 63 67(2) 61 63; Andy Roddick (USA) d. Olivier Rochus (BEL) 67(4) 76(4) 76(5) 46 63; James Blake (USA) d. Steve Darcis (BEL) 75 61.

GROUP I

Europe/Africa Zone
First Round 4-6 March

Serbia & Montenegro defeated Zimbabwe 5-0, Novi Sad, SCG; Clay (I): Novak Djokovic (SCG) d. Genius Chidzikwe (ZIM) 64 60 64; Janko Tipsarevic (SCG) d. Gwinyai Tongoona (ZIM) 63 62 61; Dusan Vemic/Nenad Zimonjic (SCG) d. Genius Chidzikwe/Gwinyai Tongoona (ZIM) 76(3) 60 63; Janko Tipsarevic (SCG) d. Zibusiso Ncube (ZIM) 60 62; Novak Djokovic (SCG) d. Pfungwa Mahefu (ZIM) 61 62.

Italy defeated Luxembourg 5-0, Luxembourg, LUX Hard (I): Daniele Bracciali (ITA) d. Gilles Muller (LUX) 76(4) 67(4) 64 64; Potito Starace (ITA) d. Mike Scheidweiler (LUX) 63 61 62; Daniele Bracciali/Giorgio Galimberti (ITA) d. Gilles Muller/Mike Scheidweiler (LUX) 64 64 67(6) 75; Potito Starace (ITA) d. Gilles Kremer (LUX) 64 62; Andreas Seppi (ITA) d. Laurent Bram (LUX) 76(4) 63.

Second Round 4-6 March

Great Britain defeated Israel 3-2, Ramat Hasharon, ISR; Hard (O): Greg Rusedski (GBR) d. Harel Levy (ISR) 64 63 60; Noam Okun (ISR) d. Alex Bogdanovic (GBR) 76(3) 62 62; Andrew Murray/David Sherwood (GBR) d. Jonathan Erlich/Andy Ram (ISR) 64 76(5) 26 76(5); Greg Rusedski (GBR) d. Noam Okun (ISR) 63 64 62; Harel Levy (ISR) d. David Sherwood (GBR) 67(1) 64 63.

Germany defeated South Africa 3-2, Doornfontein, RSA; Hard (I): Nicolas Kiefer (GER) d. Wesley Moodie (RSA) 46 67(3) 76(4) 63 62; Tommy Haas (GER) d. Wayne Ferreira (RSA) 63 60 76(3); Jeff Coetzee/Wesley Moodie (RSA) d. Nicolas Kiefer/Rainer Schuettler (GER) 63 76(4) 75; Wesley Moodie (RSA) d. Tommy Haas (GER) 67(5) 62 46 63 108; Rainer Schuettler (GER) d. Wayne Ferreira (RSA) 61 62 64.

Second Round 28-30 April

Italy defeated Morocco 4-1,Rome, ITA; Clay (O): Potito Starace (ITA) d. Mounir El Aarej (MAR) 60 36 75 60; Filippo Volandri (ITA) d. Younes El Aynaoui (MAR) 62 64 61; Daniele Bracciali/ Giorgio Galimberti (ITA) d. Younes El Aynaoui/Mehdi Tahiri (MAR) 75 61 62; Mounir El Aarej (MAR) d. Filippo Volandri (ITA) 63 16 61; Potito Starace (ITA) d. Mehdi Tahiri (MAR) 61 36 64.

29 April–1 May Belgium defeated Serbia & Montenegro 3-2, Belgrade, SCG; Clay (O): Janko Tipsarevic (SCG) d. Christophe Rochus (BEL) 26 46 75 64 61; Olivier Rochus (BEL) d. Novak Djokovic (SCG) 16 75 76(3) 61 63; Dick Norman/Kristof Vliegen (BEL) d. Dusan Vemic/Nenad Zimonjic (SCG) 63 64 36 64; Janko Tipsarevic (SCG) d. Olivier Rochus (BEL) 67(8) 36 76(3) 62 64; Kristof Vliegen (BEL) d. Novak Djokovic (SCG) 63 36 62.

Belgium, Germany, Great Britain and Italy advanced to World Group Play-offs on 23-25 September 2005.

Second Round/Play-Off 15-17 July

Luxembourg defeated Morocco 3-2, Esch sur Alzette, LUX; Hard (I): Mehdi Tahiri (MAR) d. Gilles Muller (LUX) 67(9) 64 76(1) 67(2) 64; Gilles Kremer (LUX) d. Mounir El Aarej (MAR) 63 75 64; Gilles Muller/Mike Scheidweiler (LUX) d. Mounir El Aarej/Mehdi Tahiri (MAR) 60 64 57 76(2); Gilles Muller (LUX) d. Mounir El Aarej (MAR) 63 64 67(4) 63; Mehdi Tahiri (MAR) d. Laurent Bram (LUX) 75 64.

Third Round/Play-Off 23-25 September

Israel defeated Zimbabwe 4-1, Harare, ZIM; Hard (I): Wayne Black (ZIM) d. Dudi Sela (ISR) 61 76(4) 67(2) 63; Noam Okun (ISR) d. Genius Chidzikwe (ZIM) 62 76(3) 63; Jonathan Erlich/ Andy Ram (ISR) d. Wayne Black/Gwinyai Tongoona (ZIM) 62 63 63; Dudi Sela (ISR) d. Genius Chidzikwe (ZIM) 64 64 63; Noam Okun (ISR) d. Stefan D'Almeida (ZIM) 60 62.

Morocco defeated South Africa 4-1, Khemisset, MAR; Clay (O): Mounir El Aarej (MAR) d. Justin Bower (RSA) 64 64 36 46 86; Mehdi Tahiri (MAR) d. Rik De Voest (RSA) 26 62 64 46 62; Jeff Coetzee/Chris Haggard (RSA) d. Talal Ouahabi/Mehdi Ziadi (MAR) 76(4) 67(2) 46 63 75; Mounir El Aarej (MAR) d. Rik De Voest (RSA) 63 64 75; Mehdi Tahiri (MAR) d. Justin Bower (RSA) 75 76(2).

South Africa and Zimbabwe relegated to Europe/Africa Zone Group II in 2006.

Americas Zone
First Round 4-6 March

Venezuela defeated Peru 4-1, Caracas, VEN; Hard (O): Ivan Miranda (PER) d. Jhonathan Medina (VEN) 26 75 76(4) 61; Jose De Armas (VEN) d. Sergio Rojas (PER) 61 61 63; Jose De Armas/Yohny Romero (VEN) d. Luis Horna/Ivan Miranda (PER) 63 75 62; Jose De Armas (VEN) d. Ivan Miranda (PER) 64 36 76(3) 62; Jhonathan Medina (VEN) d. Sergio Rojas (PER) 76(0) 61.

Ecuador defeated Mexico 3-2, Guanajuato, MEX; Hard (O): Giovanni Lapentti (ECU) d. Alejandro Hernandez (MEX) 63 36 67(6) 76(4) 61; Miguel Gallardo-Valles (MEX) d. Nicolas Lapentti (ECU) 46 64 62 64; Giovanni Lapentti/Nicolas Lapentti (ECU) d. Bruno Echagaray/ Santiago Gonzalez (MEX) 64 76(6) 64; Giovanni Lapentti (ECU) d. Miguel Gallardo-Valles (MEX) 63 64 36 76(5); Santiago Gonzalez (MEX) d. Carlos Avellan (ECU) 64 46 64.

Second Round 29 April–1 May

Canada defeated Venezuela 4-0, Valencia, VEN; Clay (O): Frank Dancevic (CAN) d. Yohny Romero (VEN) 64 76(4) 60; Frederic Niemeyer (CAN) d. Jose De Armas (VEN) 76(2) 61 63; Daniel Nestor/Frederic Niemeyer (CAN) d. Jose De Armas/Yohny Romero (VEN) 64 36 63 63; Robert Steckley (CAN) d. Daniel Vallverdu (VEN) 67(2) 61 64; fifth rubber not played.

Ecuador defeated Paraguay 5-0, Guayaquil, ECU; Clay (O): Giovanni Lapentti (ECU) d. Gustavo Ramirez (PAR) 60 76(3) 63; Carlos Avellan (ECU) d. Daniel Lopez (PAR) 63 60 75; Carlos Avellan/Nicolas Lapentti (ECU) d. Enzo Pigola/Juan-Carlos Ramirez (PAR) 63 64 61; Jhony De Leon (ECU) d. Juan-Carlos Ramirez (PAR) 62 61; Carlos Avellan (ECU) d. Enzo Pigola (PAR) 64 61.

Canada and Ecuador advanced to World Group Play-offs on 23-25 September 2005.

Second Round/Play-off 15-17 July

Mexico defeated Paraguay 5-0, Puebla, MEX; Hard (I): Miguel Gallardo-Valles (MEX) d. Juan-Enrique Crosa (PAR) 61 61 62; Carlos Palencia (MEX) d. Gustavo Ramirez (PAR) 64 64 62; Miguel Gallardo-Valles/Victor Romero (MEX) d. Enzo Pigola/Juan-Carlos Ramirez (PAR) 63 46 63 64; Victor Romero (MEX) d. Gustavo Ramirez (PAR) 64 64; Carlos Palencia (MEX) d. Juan-Carlos Ramirez (PAR) 62 60.

Third Round/Play-off 23-25 September

Peru defeated Paraguay 5-0, Lima, PER; Clay (O): Ivan Miranda (PER) d. Juan-Carlos Ramirez (PAR) 75 61 63; Luis Horna (PER) d. Enzo Pigola (PAR) 61 62 61; Luis Horna/Ivan Miranda (PER) d. Ricardo Gorostiaga/Juan-Carlos Ramirez (PAR) 62 61 75; Matias Silva (PER) d. Juan-Carlos Ramirez (PAR) 63 20 ret; Mauricio Echazu (PER) d. Enzo Pigola (PAR) 64 64.

Paraguay relegated to Americas Zone Group II in 2006.

Asia/Oceania Zone
First Round 4-6 March

Pakistan defeated Thailand 3-2, Lahore, PAK; Grass (O): Aisam Qureshi (PAK) d. Danai Udomchoke (THA) 62 75 67(5) 76(5); Paradorn Srichaphan (THA) d. Aqeel Khan (PAK) 64 16 76(3) 61; Aqeel Khan/Aisam Qureshi (PAK) d. Paradorn Srichaphan/Danai Udomchoke (THA) 64 57 62 76(4); Aisam Qureshi (PAK) d. Paradorn Srichaphan (THA) 75 26 64 64; Danai Udomchoke (THA) d. Shahzad Khan (PAK) 63 76(1).

Chinese Taipei defeated Japan 3-2, Tao Yuan, TPE; Hard (O): Yen-Hsun Lu (TPE) d. Gouichi Motomura (JPN) 36 63 60 46 64; Takao Suzuki (JPN) d. Yeu-Tzuoo Wang (TPE) 64 61 61; Thomas Shimada/Takao Suzuki (JPN) d. Yen-Hsun Lu/Yeu-Tzuoo Wang (TPE) 16 76(5) 64 64; Yen-Hsun Lu (TPE) d. Takao Suzuki (JPN) 57 64 63 76(1); Yeu-Tzuoo Wang (TPE) d. Gouichi Motomura (JPN) 76(4) 75 46 76(2).

Uzbekistan defeated Indonesia 3-2, Jakarta, INA; Hard (O): Denis Istomin (UZB) d. Suwandi Suwandi (INA) 63 62 64; Prima Simpatiaji (INA) d. Farrukh Dustov (UZB) 61 62 64; Suwandi Suwandi/Bonit Wiryawan (INA) d. Murad Inoyatov/Denis Istomin (UZB) 46 64 63 46 64; Farrukh Dustov (UZB) d. Suwandi Suwandi (INA) 75 75 46 26 63; Denis Istomin (UZB) d. Prima Simpatiaji (INA) 76(7) 76(5) 60.

India defeated China, P.R. 5-0, New Delhi, IND; Grass (O): Harsh Mankad (IND) d. Peng Sun (CHN) 75 63 62; Prakash Amritraj (IND) d. Yu Wang (CHN) 63 64 62; Mahesh Bhupathi/ Leander Paes (IND) d. Yu Wang/Ben-Qiang Zhu (CHN) 76(11) 63 36 61; Prakash Amritraj (IND) d. Peng Sun (CHN) 62 64; Harsh Mankad (IND) d. Hao Lu (CHN) 62 63.

Second Round 29 April–1 May

Pakistan defeated Chinese Taipei 4-1, Lahore, PAK; Grass (O): Aisam Qureshi (PAK) d. Yeu-Tzuoo Wang (TPE) 62 61 63; Yen-Hsun Lu (TPE) d. Aqeel Khan (PAK) 76(4) 46 75 76(5); Aqeel Khan/Aisam Qureshi (PAK) d. Yen-Hsun Lu/Yeu-Tzuoo Wang (TPE) 76(3) 62 75; Aisam Qureshi (PAK) d. Yen-Hsun Lu (TPE) 63 64 63; Aqeel Khan (PAK) d. Ti Chen (TPE) 67(5) 64 62.

India defeated Uzbekistan 5-0, Jaipur, IND; Grass (O): Leander Paes (IND) d. Farrukh Dustov (UZB) 76(4) 62 60; Prakash Amritraj (IND) d. Denis Istomin (UZB) 63 62 62; Mahesh Bhupathi/Leander Paes (IND) d. Murad Inoyatov/Denis Istomin (UZB) 63 64 62; Prakash Amritraj (IND) d. Farrukh Dustov (UZB) 67(4) 64 62; Harsh Mankad (IND) d Murad Inoyatov (UZB) 75 61.

India and Pakistan advanced to World Group Play-offs on 23-25 September 2005.

Second Round/Play-off 15-17 July

Japan defeated Thailand 4-1, Osaka, JPN; Carpet (I): Takao Suzuki (JPN) d. Danai Udomchoke (THA) 67(5) 64 16 75 64; Paradorn Srichaphan (THA) d. Gouichi Motomura (JPN) 64 76(2) 60; Satoshi Iwabuchi/Takao Suzuki (JPN) d. Sanchai Ratiwatana/Sonchat Ratiwatana (THA) 63 64 36 76(3); Takao Suzuki (JPN) d. Paradorn Srichaphan (THA) 62 64 64; Go Soeda (JPN) d. Sanchai Ratiwatana (THA) 63 63.

China, P.R. defeated Indonesia 4-1, Tianjin, CHN; Hard (O): Peng Sun (CHN) d. Suwandi Suwandi (INA) 63 62 64; Yu Wang (CHN) d. Prima Simpatiaji (INA) 64 60 64; Yu Wang/Xin-Yuan Yu (CHN) d. Suwandi Suwandi/Bonit Wiryawan (INA) 63 76(4) 76(2); Prima Simpatiaji (INA) d. Hao Lu (CHN) 22 ret.; Xin-Yuan Yu (CHN) d. Suwandi Suwandi (INA) 76(4) 63.

Third Round/Play-Off 23-25 September

Thailand defeated Indonesia 4-1, Bangkok, THA; Hard (O): Paradorn Srichaphan (THA) d. Sunu-Wahyu Trijati (INA) 61 64 62; Danai Udomchoke (THA) d. Prima Simpatiaji (INA) 62 63 64; Suwandi Suwandi/Bonit Wiryawan (INA) d. Sanchai Ratiwatana/Sonchat Ratiwatana (THA) 57 63 16 61 97; Paradorn Srichaphan (THA) d. Prima Simpatiaji (INA) 62 67(5) 62 76(6); Sanchai Ratiwatana (THA) d. Sunu-Wahyu Trijati (INA) 76(4) 62.

Indonesia relegated to Asia/Oceania Zone Group II in 2006.

GROUP II

Europe/Africa Zone
First Round 4-6 March

Finland defeated Ghana 5-0, Accra, GHA; Hard (O): Jarkko Nieminen (FIN) d. Salifu Mohamed (GHA) 61 62 61; Tuomas Ketola (FIN) d. Henry Adjei-Darko (GHA) 76(4) 57 61 40 ret; Lauri Kiiski/Jarkko Nieminen (FIN) d. Henry Adjei-Darko/Gunther Darkey (GHA) 36 76(3) 64 76(5); Jarkko Nieminen (FIN) d. Henry Adjei-Darko (GHA) 62 64; Tuomas Ketola (FIN) d. Salifu Mohamed (GHA) 61 63.

Bulgaria defeated Georgia 4-1,Sofia, BUL; Carpet (I): Lado Chikhladze (GEO) d. Ivaylo Traykov (BUL) 76(5) 36 76(3) 63; Todor Enev (BUL) d. Irakli Ushangishvili (GEO) 62 63 62; Yordan Kanev/Ilia Kushev (BUL) d. Lado Chikhladze/Irakli Ushangishvili (GEO) 64 36 64 64; Todor Enev (BUL) d. Lado Chikhladze (GEO) 61 62 57 64; Ivaylo Traykov (BUL) d. David Kvernadze (GEO) 62 67(7) 76(0).

Hungary defeated Monaco 4-1, Hodmezovasarhely, HUN; Hard (I): Gergely Kisgyorgy (HUN) d. Benjamin Balleret (MON) 64 26 64 46 61; Sebo Kiss (HUN) d. Emmanuel Heussner (MON) 76(8) 57 62 76(2); Gergely Kisgyorgy/Sebo Kiss (HUN) d. Benjamin Balleret/Guillaume Couillard (MON) 61 64 60; Guillaume Couillard (MON) d. Adam Kellner (HUN) 46 64 63; Denes Lukacs (HUN) d. Thomas Drouet (MON) 64 62.

Ukraine defeated Norway 4-1, Kiev, UKR; Carpet(I): Jan-Frode Andersen (NOR) d. Sergei Bubka (UKR) 76(5) 63 75; Orest Tereshchuk (UKR) d. Stian Boretti (NOR) 75 67(5) 64 67(4) 62; Mikhail Filima/Orest Tereshchuk (UKR) d. Jan-Frode Andersen/Stian Boretti (NOR) 61 63 67(4) 46 108; Mikhail Filima (UKR) d. Jan-Frode Andersen (NOR) 26 67(2) 62 76(6) 86; Sergei Bubka (UKR) d. Marius Tangen (NOR) 75 61.

Portugal defeated Estonia 4-1, Tallinn, EST; Carpet (I): Frederico Gil (POR) d. Mait Kunnap (EST) 76(7) 64 62; Leonardo Tavares (POR) d. Alti Vahkal (EST) 36 26 62 76(5) 64; Frederico Gil/Leonardo Tavares (POR) d. Mait Kunnap/Alti Vahkal (EST) 63 64 64; Andrei Luzgin (EST) d. Rui Machado (POR) 57 64 63; Diogo Rocha (POR) d. Oskar Saarne (EST) 63 62.

Algeria defeated Poland 3-2, Algiers, ALG; Clay (O): Lukasz Kubot (POL) d. Lamine Ouahab (ALG) 62 76(4) 61; Slimane Saoudi (ALG) d. Mariusz Fyrstenberg (POL) 36 63 76(2) 64; Lamine Ouahab/Slimane Saoudi (ALG) d. Mariusz Fyrstenberg/Marcin Matkowski (POL) 76(2) 64 36 63; Lukasz Kubot (POL) d. Slimane Saoudi (ALG) 57 16 62 63 60; Lamine Ouahab (ALG) d. Filip Urban (POL) 62 63 64.

Slovenia defeated Cote D'Ivoire 5-0, Kranj, SLO; Hard (I): Grega Zemlja (SLO) d. Valentin Sanon (CIV) 64 64 75; Bostjan Osabnik (SLO) d. Claude N'Goran (CIV) 61 60 26 67(5) 62; Rok Jarc/Grega Zemlja (SLO) d. Claude N'Goran/Valentin Sanon (CIV) 62 62 ret; Luka Gregorc (SLO) d. Valentin Sanon (CIV) 64 63; Rok Jarc (SLO) d. Terence Nugent (CIV) 62 60.

Latvia defeated Greece 4-1, Jurmala, LAT; Carpet (I): Andis Juska (LAT) d. Konstantinos Economidis (GRE) 76(3) 76(2) 26 62; Vasilis Mazarakis (GRE) d. Ernests Gulbis (LAT) 63 64 63; Andis Juska/Deniss Pavlovs (LAT) d. Konstantinos Economidis/Vasilis Mazarakis (GRE) 57 46 63 64 64; Andis Juska (LAT) d. Vasilis Mazarakis (GRE) 62 63 75; Deniss Pavlovs (LAT) d. Alexander Jakupovic (GRE) 61 62.

Second Round 15-17 July

Bulgaria defeated Finland 3-2, Helsinki, FIN; Clay (O): Todor Enev (BUL) d. Tuomas Ketola (FIN) 36 64 61 36 86; Jarkko Nieminen (FIN) d. Radoslav Lukaev (BUL) 76(4) 63 62; Ilia Kushev/Radoslav Lukaev (BUL) d. Lauri Kiiski/Jarkko Nieminen (FIN) 75 63 67(5) 63; Jarkko Nieminen (FIN) d. Ilia Kushev (BUL) 63 75 62; Radoslav Lukaev (BUL) d. Tuomas Ketola (FIN) 76(5) 64 61.

Ukraine defeated Hungary 3-2, Donetsk, UKR; Hard (O): Sergei Yaroshenko (UKR) d. Gergely Kisgyorgy (HUN) 63 64 67(4) 63; Orest Tereshchuk (UKR) d. Kornel Bardoczky (HUN) 64 62 36 26 63; Mikhail Filima/Orest Tereshchuk (UKR) d. Kornel Bardoczky/Gergely Kisgyorgy (HUN) 67(3) 76(2) 64 64; Kornel Bardoczky (HUN) d. Mikhail Filima (UKR) 36 76(6) 76(5); Sebo Kiss (HUN) d. Oleksandr Nedovesov (UKR) 76(4) 67(5) 64.

Portugal defeated Algeria 3-2, Lisbon, POR; Clay (O): Slimane Saoudi (ALG) d. Rui Machado (POR) 46 60 36 76(3) 64; Lamine Ouahab (ALG) d. Frederico Gil (POR) 76(2) 64 63; Frederico Gil/Leonardo Tavares (POR) d. Abdel-Hak Hameurlaine/Slimane Saoudi (ALG) 67(3) 63 61 76(3); Rui Machado (POR) d. Lamine Ouahab (ALG) 64 62 62; Frederico Gil (POR) d. Slimane Saoudi (ALG) 46 67(5) 60 62 62.

Slovenia defeated Latvia 5-0, Kranj, SLO; Clay (O): Marko Tkalec (SLO) d. Andis Juska (LAT) 61 63 64; Grega Zemlja (SLO) d. Ernests Gulbis (LAT) 57 63 61 64; Rok Jarc/Bostjan Osabnik (SLO) d. Ernests Gulbis/Andis Juska (LAT) 62 76(4) 46 62; Bostjan Osabnik (SLO) d. Deniss Pavlovs (LAT) 61 36 60; Rok Jarc (SLO) d. Janis Skroderis (LAT) 64 62.

Third Round 23-25 September

Ukraine defeated Bulgaria 4-1, Donetsk, UKR; Hard (O): Orest Tereshchuk (UKR) d. Todor Enev (BUL) 62 64 63; Radoslav Lukaev (BUL) d. Sergei Yaroshenko (UKR) 64 64 76(4); Mikhail Filima/Orest Tereshchuk (UKR) d. Ilia Kushev/Radoslav Lukaev (BUL) 64 62 76(3); Mikhail Filima (UKR) d. Todor Enev (BUL) 64 64 63; Sergei Bubka (UKR) d. Yordan Kanev (BUL) 67(7) 64 63.

Portugal defeated Slovenia 4-1, Estoril, POR; Clay (O): Frederico Gil (POR) d. Bostjan Osabnik (SLO) 76(3) 61 61; Marko Tkalec (SLO) d. Rui Machado (POR) 63 46 67(5) 61 63; Frederico Gil/Leonardo Tavares (POR) d. Rok Jarc/Grega Zemlja (SLO) 64 62 64; Rui Machado (POR) d. Grega Zemlja (SLO) 63 63 26 64; Leonardo Tavares (POR) d. Marko Tkalec (SLO) 64 75.

Portugal and Ukraine promoted to Europe/Africa Zone Group I in 2006.

Play-off 15-17 July

Georgia defeated Ghana 3-2, Accra, GHA; Hard (O): Irakli Labadze (GEO) d. Gunther Darkey (GHA) 62 62 61; Henry Adjei-Darko (GHA) d. Lado Chikhladze (GEO) 76(7) 62 62; Lado Chikhladze/Irakli Labadze (GEO) d. Henry Adjei-Darko/Gunther Darkey (GHA) 46 63 63 64; Irakli Labadze (GEO) d. Henry Adjei-Darko (GHA) 64 63 61 Salifu Mohammed (GHA) d. Irakli Ushangishvili (GEO) 46 75 63.

Norway defeated Monaco 4-1, Oslo, NOR; Clay (O): Benjamin Balleret (MON) d. Stian Boretti (NOR) 63 62 36 75; Jan Frode Andersen (NOR) d. Guillaume Couillard (MON) 62 64 67(4) 76(5); Jan Frode Andersen/Stian Boretti (NOR) d. Thomas Drouet/Emmanuel Heussner (MON) 36 62 61 62; Jan Frode Andersen (NOR) d. Benjamin Balleret (MON) 62 62 62; Stian Boretti (NOR) d. Guillaume Couillard (MON) 64 61.

Poland defeated Estonia 5-0, Gdynia, POL; Clay (O): Lukasz Kubot (POL) d. Jaak Poldma (EST) 60 61 76(7); Adam Chadaj (POL) d. Mait Kunnap (EST) 63 63 64; Mariusz Fyrstenberg/Lukasz Kubot (POL) d. Mihkel Koppel/Mait Kunnap (EST) 63 64 63; Michal Przysiezny (POL) d. Mait Kunnap (EST) 26 63 62; Adam Chadaj (POL) d. Mikk Irdoja (EST) 62 61.

Greece defeated Cote D'Ivoire 5-0, Athens, GRE; Clay (O): Konstantinos Economidis (GRE) d. Valentin Sanon (CIV) 64 63 60; Vasilis Mazarakis (GRE) d. Claude N'Goran (CIV) 76(1) 67(3) 60; Konstantinos Economidis/Vasilis Mazarakis (GRE) d. Claude N'Goran/Valentin Sanon (CIV) 36 67(8) 60 63 64; Nikos Rovas (GRE) d. Charles Irie (CIV) 61 61; Alexander Jakupovic (GRE) d. Terence Nugent (CIV) 64 36 61.

Cote d'Ivoire, Estonia, Ghana and Monaco relegated to Europe/Africa Zone Group III in 2006.

Americas Zone
First Round 4-6 March

Brazil defeated Colombia 5-0, Bogota, COL; Clay (O): Flavio Saretta (BRA) d. Pablo Gonzalez (COL) 62 46 64 61; Ricardo Mello (BRA) d. Michael Quintero (COL) 63 64 63; Andre Sa/Bruno Soares (BRA) d. Pablo Gonzalez/Michael Quintero (COL) 63 64 26 61; Andre Sa (BRA) d. Oscar Rodriguez-Sanchez (COL) 63 61; Bruno Soares (BRA) d. Sergio Ramirez (COL) 06 63 63.

Netherlands Antilles defeated Bahamas 3-2, Curacao, AHO; Hard (O): Devin Mullings (BAH) d. Rasid Winklaar (AHO) 61 63 62; Jean-Julien Rojer (AHO) d. Marvin Rolle (BAH) 62 62 75; Raoul Behr/Jean-Julien Rojer (AHO) d. Marvin Rolle/Ryan Sweeting (BAH) 64 64 64; Jean-Julien Rojer (AHO) d. Devin Mullings (BAH) 62 76(5) 63; Ryan Sweeting (BAH) d. David Josepa (AHO) 60 63.

Uruguay defeated Cuba 3-2, Havana, CUB; Hard (O): Marcel Felder (URU) d. Edgar Hernandez-Perez (CUB) 36 75 26 64 61; Ricardo Chile-Fonte (CUB) d. Pablo Cuevas (URU) 26 63 64 67(1) 63; Ricardo Chile-Fonte/Sandor Martinez-Breijo (CUB) d Marcel Felder/Martin Vilarrubi (URU) 62 62 62; Marcel Felder (URU) d. Ricardo Chile-Fonte (CUB) 36 75 62 26 61; Pablo Cuevas (URU) d. Sandor Martinez-Breijo (CUB) 62 63 63.

Dominican Republic defeated Jamaica 3-2, Kingston, JAM; Hard (O): Ryan Russell (JAM) d. Victor Estrella (DOM) 67(4) 62 62 61; Johnson Garcia (DOM) d. Scott Willinsky (JAM) 63 63 64; Victor Estrella/Johnson Garcia (DOM) d. Ryan Russell/Jermaine Smith (JAM) 64 76(5) 64; Ryan Russell (JAM) d. Johnson Garcia (DOM) 61 26 63 64; Victor Estrella (DOM) d. Damar Johnson (JAM) 46 36 64 62 63.

Second Round 15-17 July

Brazil defeated Netherlands Antilles 5-0, Santa Caterina, BRA; Clay (I): Ricardo Mello (BRA) d. David Josepa (AHO) 60 60 60; Gustavo Kuerten (BRA) d. Alexander Blom (AHO) 61 63 62; Andre Sa/Flavio Saretta (BRA) d. Raoul Behr/Alexander Blom (AHO) 61 61 64; Ricardo Mello (BRA) d. Alexander Blom (AHO) 63 41 ret.; Gustavo Kuerten (BRA) d. Raoul Behr (AHO) 60 62.

Uruguay defeated Dominican Republic 4-1, Montevideo, URU; Clay (O): Marcel Felder (URU) d. Johnson Garcia (DOM) 62 61 62; Pablo Cuevas (URU) d. Victor Estrella (DOM) 76(8) 63 63; Pablo Cuevas/Martin Vilarrubi (URU) d. Victor Estrella/Johnson Garcia (DOM) 63 62 63; Marcel Felder (URU) d. Federico Rodriguez (DOM) 64 61; Henry Estrella (DOM) d. Augusto Ricciardi-Castelli (URU) 64 26 76(2).

Final 23-25 September

Brazil defeated Uruguay 3-2, Montevideo, URU; Clay (O): Gustavo Kuerten (BRA) d. Marcel Felder (URU) 61 60 36 64; Pablo Cuevas (URU) d. Flavio Saretta (BRA) 63 36 64 62; Gustavo Kuerten/Andre Sa (BRA) d. Pablo Cuevas/Martin Vilarrubi (URU) 36 63 64 64; Ricardo Mello (BRA) d. Marcel Felder (URU) 67(5) 61 63 62; Pablo Cuevas (URU) d. Gustavo Kuerten (BRA) 76(5) ret.

Brazil promoted to Americas Zone Group I in 2006.

Play-off 15-17 July

Colombia defeated Bahamas 5-0, Bogota, COL; Clay (O): Pablo Gonzalez (COL) d. Marvin Rolle (BAH) 36 62 62 36 62; Alejandro Falla (COL) d. Devin Mullings (BAH) 64 62 63; Alejandro Falla/Carlos Salamanca (COL) d. Marvin Rolle/Ryan Sweeting (BAH) 75 61 63; Alejandro Falla (COL) d. Ryan Sweeting (BAH) 64 64; Michael Quintero (COL) d. H'Cone Thompson (BAH) 61 61.

Jamaica defeated Cuba 3-1, Kingston, JAM; Hard (O): Ryan Russell (JAM) d. Edgar Hernandez-Perez (CUB) 60 62 61; Damar Johnson (JAM) d. Ricardo Chile-Fonte (CUB) 63 76(6) 64; Ricardo Chile-Fonte/Sandor Martinez-Breijo (CUB) d. Damar Johnson/Ryan Russell (JAM) 63 64 36 46 63; Ryan Russell (JAM) d. Ricardo Chile-Fonte (CUB) 36 76(2) 76(6) 23 ret; fifth rubber not played.

Bahamas and Cuba relegated to Americas Zone Group III in 2006.

Asia/Oceania Zone
First Round 4-6 March

New Zealand defeated Kazakhstan 4-1, Auckland, NZL; Hard (I): Mark Nielsen (NZL) d. Dmitri Makeyev (KAZ) 60 62 63; GD Jones (NZL) d. Alexey Kedriouk (KAZ) 63 64 64; Mark Nielsen/Matt Prentice (NZL) d. Alexey Kedriouk/Dmitri Makeyev (KAZ) 63 62 62; Alexey Kedriouk (KAZ) d. Jose Statham (NZL) 64 75; GD Jones (NZL) d. Stanislav Buykov (KAZ) 61 60.

Kuwait defeated Iran 4-1, Tehran, IRI; Clay (O): Abdullah Magdas (KUW) d. Ashkan Shokoofi (IRI) 76(7) 75 63; Mohammed Al Ghareeb (KUW) d. Anoosha Shahgholi (IRI) 75 76(5) 63; Mohammed Al Ghareeb/Mohamed-Khaliq Siddiq (KUW) d. Ashkan Shokoofi/Akbar Taheri (IRI) 61 64 75; Shahab Hassani-Nafez (IRI) d. Mohammad Ahmad (KUW) 62 75; Abdullah Magdas (KUW) d. Anoosha Shahgholi (IRI) 63 63.

Pacific Oceania defeated Lebanon 3-2, Lautoka, FIJ; Hard (O): Michael Leong (POC) d. Patrick Chucri (LIB) 63 26 63 57 30 ret; Juan Sebastien Langton (POC) d. Karim Alayli (LIB) 67(6) 63 61 75; Patrick Chucri/Jicham Zaatini (LIB) d. Brett Baudinet/Juan Sebastien Langton (POC) 63 76(0) 76(4); Michael Leong (POC) d. Jicham Zaatini (LIB) 75 67(14) 63 46 62; Patrick Chucri (LIB) d. Brett Baudinet (POC) 64 26 62.

Korea, Rep. defeated Philippines 3-2, Manila, PHI; Clay (I): Patrick Tierro (PHI) d. Hyun-Joon Suk (KOR) 75 75 64; Woong-Sun Jun (KOR) d. Johnny Arcilla (PHI) 64 36 76(7) 46 64; Hee-Seok Chung/Dong-Hyun Kim (KOR) d. Johnny Arcilla/Joseph Victorino (PHI) 64 60 60; Woong-Sun Jun (KOR) d. Patrick Tierro (PHI) 63 63 63; Johnny Arcilla (PHI) d. Hyun-Joon Suk (KOR) 62 75.

Second Round 15-17 July

New Zealand defeated Kuwait 3-2, Auckland, NZL; Hard (I): Mark Nielsen (NZL) d. Abdullah Magdas (KUW) 76(1) 16 64 61; GD Jones (NZL) d. Mohammed Al Ghareeb (KUW) 36 64 75 62; Daniel King-Turner/Mark Nielsen (NZL) d. Mohammed Al Ghareeb/Mohamed-Khaliq Siddiq (KUW) 76(4) 64 64; Mohammed Al Ghareeb (KUW) d. Adam Thompson (NZL) 75 63; Abdullah Magdas (KUW) d. Daniel King-Turner (NZL) 76(4) 57 63.

Korea, Rep. defeated Pacific Oceania 5-0, Seoul, KOR; Hard (O): Sun-Yong Kim (KOR) d. Michael Leong (POC) 60 36 64 63; Woong-Sun Jun (KOR) d. West Nott (POC) 75 64 61; Woong-Sun Jun/Oh-Hee Kwon (KOR) d. Brett Baudinet/Juan Sebastien Langton (POC) 61 60 64; Jae-Sung An (KOR) d. Michael Leong (POC) 64 63; Sun-Yong Kim (KOR) d. Juan Sebastien Langton (POC) 64 63.

Final 23-25 September

Korea, Rep. defeated New Zealand 3-2, Auckland, NZL; Hard (I): Mark Nielsen (NZL) d. Kyu-Tae Im (KOR) 06 46 64 60 52 ret;Hyung-Taik Lee (KOR) d. Daniel King-Turner (NZL) 61 76(5) 61; Oh-Hee Kwon/Hyung-Taik Lee (KOR) d. Daniel King-Turner/Mark Nielsen (NZL) 62 62 62; Hyung-Taik Lee (KOR) d. Mark Nielsen (NZL) 62 76(8) 63; Jose "Rubin" Statham (NZL) d. Sun-Yong Kim (KOR) 64 64.

Korea, Rep. promoted to Asia/Oceania Zone Group I in 2006.

Play-off 15-17 July

Kazakhstan defeated Iran 3-2, Tehran, IRI; Clay (O): Alexey Kedriouk (KAZ) d. Shahab Hassani-Nafez (IRI) 75 61 62; Ashkan Shokoofi (IRI) d. Dmitri Makeyev (KAZ) 63 64 60; Alexey Kedriouk/Anton Tsymbalov (KAZ) d. Ramin Raziyani/Ashkan Shokoofi (IRI) 64 62 76(4); Alexey Kedriouk (KAZ) d. Ashkan Shokoofi (IRI) 63 61 64; Anoosha Shahgholi (IRI) d. Dmitri Makeyev (KAZ) 63 67(5) 64.

Lebanon defeated Philippines 3-2, Beirut, LIB; Clay (O): Patrick Chucri (LIB) d. Johnny Arcilla (PHI) 62 62 62; Patrick Tierro (PHI) d. Karim Alayli (LIB) 63 36 64 16 75; Karim Alayli/Patrick Chucri (LIB) d. Adelo Abadia/Johnny Arcilla (PHI) 26 63 46 64 64; Patrick Tierro (PHI) d. Patrick Chucri (LIB) 67(5) 67(8) 61 64 75; Karim Alayli (LIB) d. Johnny Arcilla (PHI) 62 76(5) 61.

Iran and Philippines relegated to Asia/Oceania Zone Group III in 2006.

GROUP III

Europe/Africa Zone – Venue I

Date: 27 April-1 May **Venue:** Cairo, Egypt **Surface:** Clay (O)
Group A: Denmark, Kenya, Macedonia, F.Y.R., Namibia
Group B: Bosnia/Herzegovina, Egypt, Lithuania, Madagascar

Group A

27 April Denmark defeated Kenya 3-0: Mik Ledvonova (DEN) d. Christian Vitulli (KEN) 63 63; Frederik Nielsen (DEN) d. Allan Cooper (KEN) 60 64; Frederik Nielsen/Morgan Thempler (DEN) d. Willis Mbandi/Christian Vitulli (KEN) 62 62.

Macedonia, F.Y.R. defeated Namibia 3-0: Predrag Rusevski (MKD) d. Johan Theron (NAM) 60 63; Lazar Magdincev (MKD) d. Jurgens Strydom (NAM) 64 60; Lazar Magdincev/Predrag Rusevski (MKD) d. Henrico Du Plessis/Jurgens Strydom (NAM) 61 61.

28 April Denmark defeated Namibia 3-0: Mik Ledvonova (DEN) d. Johan Theron (NAM) 62 62; Frederik Nielsen (DEN) d. Jurgens Strydom (NAM) 60 62; Frederik Nielsen/Morgan Thempler (DEN) d. Henrico Du Plessis/Jean-Pierre Huish (NAM) 62 62.

Macedonia, F.Y.R. defeated Kenya 3-0: Predrag Rusevski (MKD) d. Willis Mbandi (KEN) 60 60; Lazar Magdincev (MKD) d. Allan Cooper (KEN) 61 61; Dimitar Grabulovski/Predrag Rusevski (MKD) d. Allan Cooper/Maurice Wamukowa (KEN) 62 63.

29 April Macedonia, F.Y.R. defeated Denmark 3-0: Predrag Rusevski (MKD) d. Mik Ledvonova (DEN) 57 63 62; Lazar Magdincev (MKD) d. Frederik Nielsen (DEN) 61 76(3); Lazar Magdincev/Predrag Rusevski (MKD) d. Frederik Nielsen/Morgan Thempler (DEN) 62 63.

Namibia defeated Kenya 2-1: Christian Vitulli (KEN) d. Johan Theron (NAM) 61 46 63; Jurgens Strydom (NAM) d. Allan Cooper (KEN) 67(7) 63 63; Henrico Du Plessis/Jurgens Strydom (NAM) d. Allan Cooper/Christian Vitulli (KEN) 67(4) 62 64.

Group B

27 April Egypt defeated Madagascar 3-0: Mohamed Maamoun (EGY) d. Jacob Rasolondrazana (MAD) 61 62; Karim Maamoun (EGY) d. Germain Rasolondrazana (MAD) 62 60; Omar Hedayet/Mohamed Nashaat (EGY) d. Thierry Rajaobelina/Germain Rasolondrazana (MAD) 62 76(4).

Bosnia/Herzegovina defeated Lithuania 2-1: Bojan Vujic (BIH) d. Rolandas Murashka (LTU) 63 36 60; Daniel Lencina (LTU) d. Ivan Dodig (BIH) 64 76(5); Ivan Dodig/Bojan Vujic (BIH) d. Daniel Lencina/Rolandas Murashka (LTU) 64 62.

28 April Egypt defeated Bosnia/Herzegovina 3-0: Mohamed Maamoun (EGY) d. Bojan Vujic (BIH) 62 62; Karim Maamoun (EGY) d. Ivan Dodig (BIH) 57 62 64; Karim Maamoun/Mohamed Maamoun (EGY) d. Ivan Dodig/Bojan Vujic (BIH) 61 64.

Lithuania defeated Madagascar 3-0: Gvidas Sabeckis (LTU) d. Thierry Rajaobelina (MAD) 61 63; Daniel Lencina (LTU) d. Germain Rasolondrazana (MAD) 63 63; Rolandas Murashka/Gvidas Sabeckis (LTU) d. Antso Rakotondramanga/Germain Rasolondrazana (MAD) 62 76(7).

29 April Egypt defeated Lithuania 2-1: Rolandas Murashka (LTU) d. Mohamed Maamoun (EGY) 06 61 63; Karim Maamoun (EGY) d. Daniel Lencina (LTU) 62 76(3); Karim Maamoun/Mohamed Maamoun (EGY) d. Rolandas Murashka/Gvidas Sabeckis (LTU) 46 76(7) 64.

Bosnia/Herzegovina defeated Madagascar 2-1: Bojan Vujic (BIH) d. Antso Rakotondramanga (MAD) 62 62; Ivan Dodig (BIH) d. Jacob Rasolondrazana (MAD) 63 36 63; Thierry Rajaobelina/Germain Rasolondrazana (MAD) d. Aleksandar Maric/Ugljesa Ostojic (BIH) 63 63.

Play-off for 1st-4th positions:

Results carried forward: **Macedonia, F.Y.R. defeated Denmark 3-0;**
Egypt defeated Bosnia-Herzegovina 3-0.

30 April Macedonia, F.Y.R. defeated Bosnia/Herzegovina 3-0: Predrag Rusevski (MKD) d. Bojan Vujic (BIH) 62 60; Lazar Magdincev (MKD) d. Ivan Dodig (BIH) 62 62; Lazar Magdincev/Predrag Rusevski (MKD) d. Aleksandar Maric/Ugljesa Ostojic (BIH) 61 75.

Egypt defeated Denmark 2-1: Mohamed Maamoun (EGY) d. Mik Ledvonova (DEN) 62 63; Frederik Nielsen (DEN) d. Karim Maamoun (EGY) 64 63; Karim Maamoun/Mohamed Maamoun (EGY) d. Frederik Nielsen/Morgan Thempler (DEN) 62 26 63.

1 May Macedonia, F.Y.R. defeated Egypt 2-1: Omar Hedayet (EGY) d. Dimitar Grabulovski (MKD) 63 63; Predrag Rusevski (MKD) d. Mohamed Nashaat (EGY) 64 62; Lazar Magdincev/Predrag Rusevski (MKD) d. Mohamed Maamoun/Mohamed Nashaat (EGY) 26 64 63.

Denmark defeated Bosnia/Herzegovina 2-1: Jacob Melskens (DEN) d. Aleksandar Maric (BIH) 64 26 64; Frederik Nielsen (DEN) d. Ugljesa Ostojic (BIH) 61 60; Aleksandar Maric/Bojan Vujic (BIH) d. Jacob Melskens/Morgan Thempler (DEN) 62 76(2).

Play-off for 5th-8th Positions:

Results carried forward: **Namibia defeated Kenya 2-1; Lithuania defeated Madagascar 3-0,**

30 April Namibia defeated Madagascar 2-1: Johan Theron (NAM) d. Thierry Rajaobelina (MAD) 75 26 63; Jurgens Strydom (NAM) d. Germain Rasolondrazana (MAD) 62 63; Antso Rakotondramanga/Germain Rasolondrazana (MAD) d. Henrico Du Plessis/Jurgens Strydom (NAM) 63 36 64.

Lithuania defeated Kenya 3-0: Gvidas Sabeckis (LTU) d. Christian Vitulli (KEN) 63 67(4) 64; Daniel Lencina (LTU) d. Allan Cooper (KEN) 61 57 97; Arturas Gotovskis/Rolandas Murashka (LTU) d. Christian Vitulli/Maurice Wamukowa (KEN) 36 62 60

1 May Lithuania defeated Namibia 2-1: Jean-Pierre Huish (NAM) d. Arturas Gotovskis (LTU) 61 63; Rolandas Murashka (LTU) d. Jurgens Strydom (NAM) 62 62; Daniel Lencina/Rolandas Murashka (LTU) d. Jean-Pierre Huish/Jurgens Strydom (NAM) 76(6) 61.

Madagascar defeated Kenya 3-0: Antso Rakotondramanga (MAD) d. Maurice Wamukowa (KEN) 63 75; Germain Rasolondrazana (MAD) d. Willis Mbandi (KEN) 62 61; Antso Rakotondramanga/Germain Rasolondrazana (MAD) d. Willis Mbandi/Maurice Wamukowa (KEN) 64 62.

Final Positions: 1. Macedonia, F.Y.R., 2. Egypt, 3. Denmark, 4. Bosnia/Herzegovina, 5. Lithuania, 6. Namibia, 7. Madagascar, 8. Kenya.

Macedonia, F.Y.R. and Egypt promoted to Europe/Africa Zone Group II in 2006. Madagascar and Kenya relegated to Europe/Africa Zone Group IV in 2006.

Europe/Africa Zone – Venue II

Date: 13-17 July **Venue:** Dublin, Ireland **Surface:** Carpet (O)
Group A: Armenia, Iceland, Ireland, Nigeria
Group B: Cyprus, San Marino, Tunisia, Turkey

Group A

13 July Ireland defeated Nigeria 3-0: Louk Sorensen (IRL) d. Abdul-Mumin Babalola (NGR) 60 61; Kevin Sorensen (IRL) d. Jonathan Igbinovia (NGR) 63 63; Conor Niland/David O'Connell (IRL) d. Jonathan Igbinovia/Damisa Robinson (NGR) 62 64.

Armenia defeated Iceland 2-1: Harutyun Sofyan (ARM) d. Andri Jonsson (ISL) 62 64; Arnar Sigurdsson (ISL) d. Sargis Sargsian (ARM) 75 06 63; Sargis Sargsian/Harutyun Sofyan (ARM) d. Raj-Kumar Bonifacius/Arnar Sigurdsson (ISL) 61 64.

14 July Ireland defeated Armenia 3-0: Louk Sorensen (IRL) d. Harutyun Sofyan (ARM) 63 63; Kevin Sorensen (IRL) d. Sargis Sargsian (ARM) 63 63; Conor Niland/David O'Connell (IRL) d. Sargis Sargsian/Harutyun Sofyan (ARM) 75 16 75.

Nigeria defeated Iceland 3-0: Abdul-Mumin Babalola (NGR) d. Andri Jonsson (ISL) 62 60; Jonathan Igbinovia (NGR) d. Arnar Sigurdsson (ISL) 76(6) 62; Abdul-Mumin Babalola/Lawal Shehu (NGR) d. Andri Jonsson/Arnar Sigurdsson (ISL) 75 76(7).

15 July Ireland defeated Iceland 3-0: Conor Niland (IRL) d. Andri Jonsson (ISL) 60 60; Kevin Sorensen (IRL) d. Raj-Kumar Bonifacius (ISL) 62 61; Conor Niland/David O'Connell (IRL) d. David Halldorsson/Andri Jonsson (ISL) 62 60.

Armenia defeated Nigeria 2-1: Abdul-Mumin Babalola (NGR) d. Harutyun Sofyan (ARM) 57 61 64; Sargis Sargsian (ARM) d. Jonathan Igbinovia (NGR) 62 76(7); Sargis Sargsian/Harutyun Sofyan (ARM) d. Jonathan Igbinovia/Damisa Robinson (NGR) 63 63.

Group B

13 July Tunisia defeated San Marino 3-0: Heithem Abid (TUN) d. Domenico Vicini (SMR) 67(6) 75 62; Malek Jaziri (TUN) d. Diego Zonzini (SMR) 60 63; Heithem Abid/Malek Jaziri (TUN) d. William Forcellini/Christian Rosti (SMR) 60 75.

Cyprus defeated Turkey 2-1: Fotos Kallias (CYP) d. Baris Erguden (TUR) 76(7) 61; Marcos Baghdatis (CYP) d. Haluk Akkoyun (TUR) 63 61; Haluk Akkoyun/Esat Tanik (TUR) d. Fotos Kallias/Demetrios Leontis (CYP) 64 57 63.

14 July Cyprus defeated Tunisia 3-0: Fotos Kallias (CYP) d. Heithem Abid (TUN) 64 61; Marcos Baghdatis (CYP) d. Malek Jaziri (TUN) 61 63; Marcos Baghdatis/Demetrios Leontis (CYP) d. Wael Kilani/Fares Zaier (TUN) 76(5) 63.

Turkey defeated San Marino 3-0: Baris Erguden (TUR) d. Domenico Vicini (SMR) 76(3) 64; Haluk Akkoyun (TUR) d. William Forcellini (SMR) 63 62; Haluk Akkoyun/Esat Tanik (TUR) d. William Forcellini/Christian Rosti (SMR) 76(4) 62.

15 July Tunisia defeated Turkey 2-1: Heithem Abid (TUN) d. Esat Tanik (TUR) 62 63; Haluk Akkoyun (TUR) d. Malek Jaziri (TUN) 63 64; Heithem Abid/Malek Jaziri (TUN) d. Haluk Akkoyun/Baris Erguden (TUR) 64 36 61.

Cyprus defeated San Marino 3-0: Christopher Koutrouzas (CYP) d. Christian Rosti (SMR) 63 64; Fotos Kallias (CYP) d. Diego Zonzini (SMR) 60 60; Marcos Baghdatis/Demetrios Leontis (CYP) d. William Forcellini/Diego Zonzini (SMR) 61 61.

Play-Off for 1st-4th Positions:

Results carried forward: **Ireland defeated Armenia 3-0; Cyprus defeated Tunisia 3-0.**

16 July Cyprus defeated Ireland 2-1: Conor Niland (IRL) d. Fotos Kallias (CYP) 64 36 60; Marcos Baghdatis (CYP) d. Kevin Sorensen (IRL) 62 46 60; Marcos Baghdatis/Demetrios Leontis (CYP) d. Conor Niland/David O'Connell (IRL) 46 60 61.

Armenia defeated Tunisia 2-1: Heithem Abid (TUN) d. Harutyun Sofyan (ARM) 76(3) 75; Sargis Sargsian (ARM) d. Malek Jaziri (TUN) 64 61; Sargis Sargsian/Harutyun Sofyan (ARM) d. Malek Jaziri/Wael Kilani (TUN) 64 63.

17 July Ireland defeated Tunisia 3-0: Louk Sorensen (IRL) d. Wael Kilani (TUN) 61 62; Kevin Sorensen (IRL) d. Malek Jaziri (TUN) 62 75; David O'Connell/Kevin Sorensen (IRL) d. Wael Kilani/Fares Zaier (TUN) 62 57 62.

Cyprus defeated Armenia 2-1: Fotos Kallias (CYP) d. Harutyun Sofyan (ARM) 60 61; Marcos Baghdatis (CYP) d. Hayk Zohranyan (ARM) 63 61; Harutyun Sofyan/Hayk Zohranyan (ARM) d. Christopher Koutrouzas/Demetrios Leontis (CYP) 76(4) 62

Play-off for 5th-8th Positions:

Results carried forward: **Nigeria defeated Iceland 3-0; Turkey defeated San Marino 3-0.**

16 July Nigeria defeated Turkey 2-1: Abdul-Mumin Babalola (NGR) d. Baris Erguden (TUR) 64 62; Haluk Akkoyun (TUR) d. Jonathan Igbinovia (NGR) 76(5) 16 64; Abdul-Mumin Babalola/Lawal Shehu (NGR) d. Haluk Akkoyun/Esat Tanik (TUR) 64 64.

Iceland defeated San Marino 2-1: Domenico Vicini (SMR) d. Raj-Kumar Bonifacius (ISL) 63 76(5); Arnar Sigurdsson (ISL) d. William Forcellini (SMR) 61 60; Andri Jonsson/Arnar Sigurdsson (ISL) d. Christian Rosti/Domenico Vicini (SMR) 63 75.

17 July Nigeria defeated San Marino 3-0: Abdul-Mumin Babalola (NGR) d. William Forcellini (SMR) 61 62; Jonathan Igbinovia (NGR) d. Diego Zonzini (SMR) 61 61; Abdul-Mumin Babalola/Lawal Shehu (NGR) d. Domenico Vicini/Diego Zonzini (SMR) 76(6) 75.

Turkey defeated Iceland 2-1: Baris Erguden (TUR) d. Raj-Kumar Bonifacius (ISL) 64 76(3); Arnar Sigurdsson (ISL) d. Haluk Akkoyun (TUR) 62 76(2); Haluk Akkoyun/Baris Erguden (TUR) d. Andri Jonsson/Arnar Sigurdsson (ISL) 62 76(4).

Final Positions: 1. Cyprus, 2. Ireland, 3. Armenia, 4. Tunisia, 5. Nigeria, 6. Turkey, 7. Iceland, 8. San Marino.

Cyprus and Ireland promoted to Europe/Africa Zone Group II in 2006. Iceland and San Marino relegated to Europe/Africa Zone Group IV in 2006.

Americas Zone

Date: 2-6 March **Venue:** La Paz, Bolivia **Surface:** Clay (O)
Group A: Bolivia, Haiti, Honduras, St. Lucia.
Group B: El Salvador, Guatemala, Panama, Puerto Rico.

Group A

2 March Haiti defeated St. Lucia 2-1: Bertrand Madsen (HAI) d. Vernon Lewis (LCA) 63 64; Olivier Claude Sajous (HAI) d. Sirsean Arlain (LCA) 62 61; Kane Easter/Vernon Lewis (LCA) d. Gael Gaetjens/Iphton Louis (HAI) 64 64.

Bolivia defeated Honduras 3-0: Jose Antelo (BOL) d. Jose Moncada (HON) 75 62; Mauricio Estivariz (BOL) d. Calton Alvarez (HON) 62 75; Jose Antelo/Mauricio Estivariz (BOL) d. Carlos Caceres/Jose Moncada (HON) 26 75 62.

3 March Bolivia defeated Haiti 3-0: Jose Antelo (BOL) d. Bertrand Madsen (HAI) 36 63 64; Mauricio Estivariz (BOL) d. Olivier Claude Sajous (HAI) 61 76(8); Mario Salinas/Jorge Villanueva (BOL) d. Iphton Louis/Bertrand Madsen (HAI) 62 67(2) 108.

Honduras defeated St. Lucia 3-0: Jose Moncada (HON) d. Alberton Richelieu (LCA) 64 75; Calton Alvarez (HON) d. Vernon Lewis (LCA) 61 64; Carlos Caceres/Jose Moncada (HON) d. Kane Easter/Vernon Lewis (LCA) 63 26 75.

4 March Haiti defeated Honduras 3-0: Bertrand Madsen (HAI) d. Jose Moncada (HON) 63 64; Olivier Claude Sajous (HAI) d. Calton Alvarez (HON) 76(5) 64; Gael Gaetjens/Iphton Louis (HAI) d. Carlos Caceres/Jose Moncada (HON) 63 63.

Bolivia defeated St. Lucia 3-0: Jose Antelo (BOL) d. Kane Easter (LCA) 60 63; Mauricio Estivariz (BOL) d. Sirsean Arlain (LCA) 60 61; Mario Salinas/Jorge Villanueva (BOL) d. Sirsean Arlain/Kane Easter (LCA) 63 63.

Group B

2 March Guatemala defeated Panama 3-0: Cristian Paiz (GUA) d. Alberto Gonzalez (PAN) 63 62; Jacobo Chavez (GUA) d. Augusto Alvarado (PAN) 61 62; Manuel Chavez/Luis Perez-Chete (GUA) d. Braen Aneiros-Romero/Alberto Gonzalez (PAN) 62 64.

Puerto Rico defeated El Salvador 2-1: Jorge Rangel (PUR) d. Manuel-Antonio Tejada-Ruiz (ESA) 61 64; Rafael Arevalo-Gonzalez (ESA) d. Gabriel Montilla (PUR) 62 60; Gilberto Alvarez/ Gabriel Montilla (PUR) d. Rafael Arevalo-Gonzalez/Manuel-Antonio Tejada-Ruiz (ESA) 63 64.

3 March Guatemala defeated Puerto Rico 2-1: Cristian Paiz (GUA) d. Jorge Rangel (PUR) 62 61; Jacobo Chavez (GUA) d. Gabriel Montilla (PUR) 63 62; Gilberto Alvarez/Gabriel Montilla (PUR) d. Manuel Chavez/Luis Perez-Chete (GUA) 57 76(5) 64.

El Salvador defeated Panama 3-0: Manuel-Antonio Tejada-Ruiz (ESA) d. Juan Jose Fuentes (PAN) 62 62; Rafael Arevalo-Gonzalez (ESA) d. Alberto Gonzalez (PAN) 62 61; Rafael Arevalo-Gonzalez/ Manuel-Antonio Tejada-Ruiz (ESA) d. Juan Jose Fuentes/Alberto Gonzalez (PAN) 63 63.

4 March Guatemala defeated El Salvador 2-1: Cristian Paiz (GUA) d. Manuel-Antonio Tejada-Ruiz (ESA) 63 64; Rafael Arevalo-Gonzalez (ESA) d. Jacobo Chavez (GUA) 63 61; Manuel Chavez/ Luis Perez-Chete (GUA) d. Rafael Arevalo-Gonzalez/Manuel-Antonio Tejada-Ruiz (ESA) 64 64.

Puerto Rico defeated Panama 2-1: Gilberto Alvarez (PUR) d. Braen Aneiros-Romero (PAN) 64 62; Alberto Gonzalez (PAN) d. Gabriel Montilla (PUR) 63 75; Gilberto Alvarez/Gabriel Montilla (PUR) d. Juan Jose Fuentes/Alberto Gonzalez (PAN) 63 62.

Play-Off for 1st-4th Positions:

Results carried forward: **Bolivia defeated Haiti 3-0; Guatemala defeated Puerto Rico 2-1.**

5 March Bolivia defeated Puerto Rico 3-0: Jose Antelo (BOL) d. Gilberto Alvarez (PUR) 62 62; Mauricio Estivariz (BOL) d. Gabriel Montilla (PUR) 75 62; Jose Antelo/Mauricio Estivariz (BOL) d. Gilberto Alvarez/Gabriel Montilla (PUR) 57 63 62.

Guatemala defeated Haiti 3-0: Luis Perez-Chete (GUA) d. Bertrand Madsen (HAI) 64 26 64; Cristian Paiz (GUA) d. Olivier Claude Sajous (HAI) 75 62; Jacobo Chavez/Luis Perez-Chete (GUA) d. Gael Gaetjens/Iphton Louis (HAI) 64 62

6 March Guatemala defeated Bolivia 3-0: Luis Perez-Chete (GUA) d. Jose Antelo (BOL) 60 75; Cristian Paiz (GUA) d. Mauricio Estivariz (BOL) 76(4) 63; Jacobo Chavez/Manuel Chavez (GUA) d. Mario Salinas/Jorge Villanueva (BOL) 26 64 62.

Puerto Rico defeated Haiti 2-0: Gilberto Alvarez (PUR) d. Gael Gaetjens (HAI) 60 60; Jorge Rangel (PUR) d. Olivier Claude Sajous (HAI) 63 63; Doubles not played.

Play-Off for 5th-8th Positions:

Results carried forward: **Honduras defeated St. Lucia 3-0; El Salvador defeated Panama 3-0.**

5 March Honduras defeated Panama 2-1: Jose Moncada (HON) d. Braen Aneiros-Romero (PAN) 36 63 62; Alberto Gonzalez (PAN) d. Calton Alvarez (HON) 75 64; Carlos Caceres/Jose Moncada (HON) d. Braen Aneiros-Romero/Alberto Gonzalez (PAN) 64 76(3).

El Salvador defeated St. Lucia 3-0: Manuel-Antonio Tejada-Ruiz (ESA) d. Vernon Lewis (LCA) 36 60 62; Rafael Arevalo-Gonzalez (ESA) d. Sirsean Arlain (LCA) 61 60; Rafael Arevalo-Gonzalez/ Manuel-Antonio Tejada-Ruiz (ESA) d. Kane Easter/Alberton Richelieu (LCA) 61 64.

6 March Honduras defeated El Salvador 2-0: Carlos Caceres (HON) d. Marcelo Arevalo (ESA) 61 61; Jose Moncada (HON) d. Manuel-Antonio Tejada-Ruiz (ESA) 64 67(3) 61; Doubles not played.

Panama defeated St. Lucia 2-0: Braen Aneiros-Romero (PAN) d. Kane Easter (LCA) 76(8) 46 64; Alberto Gonzalez (PAN) d. Sirsean Arlain (LCA) 63 63; Doubles not played.

Final Positions: 1. Guatemala, 2. Bolivia, 3. Puerto Rico, 4. Haiti, 5. Honduras, 6. El Salvador, 7. Panama, 8. St Lucia.

Guatemala and Bolivia promoted to Americas Zone Group II in 2006.
Panama and St. Lucia relegated to Americas Group IV in 2006.

Asia/Oceania Zone

Date: 13-17 July **Venue:** Causeway Bay, Hong Kong, China **Surface:** Hard (O)
Group A: Hong Kong China; Malaysia, Saudi Arabia, Tajikistan
Group B: Bahrain, Qatar, Sri Lanka, Vietnam

Group A

13 July Hong Kong, China defeated Saudi Arabia 3-0: Martin Sayer (HKG) d. Fahad Al Saad (KSA) 62 62; Hiu-Tung Yu (HKG) d. Omar Al Thagib (KSA) 61 60; Brian Hung/Martin Sayer (HKG) d. Fahad Al Saad/Bager Bokhleaf (KSA) 62 62.

Malaysia defeated Tajikistan 3-0: Selvam Veerasingam (MAS) d. Mirkhusein Yakhyaev (TJK) 61 60; Yew-Ming Si (MAS) d. Dilshod Sharifi (TJK) 63 75; Nikesh Singh Panthlia/Adrian Tan (MAS) d. Dilshod Sharifi/Mirkhusein Yakhyaev (TJK) 64 61.

14 July Hong Kong, China defeated Malaysia 3-0: Wayne Wong (HKG) d. Selvam Veerasingam (MAS) 67(5) 63 64; Hiu-Tung Yu (HKG) d. Yew-Ming Si (MAS) 36 76(2) 75; Brian Hung/Martin Sayer (HKG) d. Nikesh Singh Panthlia/Adrian Tan (MAS) 61 61.

Saudi Arabia defeated Tajikistan 2-1: Fahad Al Saad (KSA) d. Mirkhusein Yakhyaev (TJK) 62 62; Dilshod Sharifi (TJK) d. Omar Al Thagib (KSA) 60 46 63; Badar Al Megayel/Fahad Al Saad (KSA) d. Dilshod Sharifi/Mansour Yakhyaev (TJK) 62 64.

15 July Hong Kong, China defeated Tajikistan 3-0: Martin Sayer (HKG) d. Mirkhusein Yakhyaev (TJK) 60 62; Brian Hung (HKG) d. Dilshod Sharifi (TJK) 60 61; Brian Hung/Martin Sayer (HKG) d. Rahmatullo Rajabaliev/Mirkhusein Yakhyaev (TJK) 60 61.

Malaysia defeated Saudi Arabia 2-1; Fahad Al Saad (KSA) d. Adrian Tan (MAS) 64 62; Yew-Ming Si (MAS) d. Omar Al Thagib (KSA) 62 64; Yew-Ming Si/Selvam Veerasingam (MAS) d. Badar Al Megayel/Fahad Al Saad (KSA) 61 63.

Group B

13 July Sri Lanka defeated Qatar 3-0: Harshana Godamanne (SRI) d. Sultan-Khalfan Al Alawi (QAT) 62 61; Renouk Wijemanne (SRI) d. Mohammed Abdulla (QAT) 64 60; Harshana Godamanne/Oshada Wijemanne (SRI) d. Mohammed Abdulla/Abdulla Hajji (QAT) 61 61.

Vietnam defeated Bahrain 2-1: Abdul-Rahman Shehab (BRN) d. Quang-Huy Ngo (VIE) 64 63; Minh-Quan Do (VIE) d. Mohammed Abdul-Latif (BRN) 60 62; Minh-Quan Do/Quoc-Khanh Le (VIE) d. Mohammed Abdul-Latif/Abdul-Rahman Shehab (BRN) 63 62.

14 July Vietnam defeated Qatar 3-0: Quang-Huy Ngo (VIE) d. Sultan-Khalfan Al Alawi (QAT) 63 76(5); Minh-Quan Do (VIE) d. Mohammed Abdulla (QAT) 61 62; Quoc-Khanh Le/Thanh-Hoang Tran (VIE) d. Mohammed Abdulla/Abdulla Hajji (QAT) 62 61.

Sri Lanka defeated Bahrain 3-0: Harshana Godamanne (SRI) d. Abdul-Rahman Shehab (BRN) 61 64; Renouk Wijemanne (SRI) d. Khaled Al Thawadi (BRN) 62 64; Rajeev Rajapakse/Oshada Wijemanne (SRI) d. Mohammed Abdul-Latif/Abdul-Latif Al Murraghi (BRN) 75 64.

15 July Bahrain defeated Qatar 2-1: Abdul-Rahman Shehab (BRN) d. Sultan-Khalfan Al Alawi (QAT) 75 63; Mohammed Abdulla (QAT) d. Khaled Al Thawadi (BRN) 62 36 86; Mohammed Abdul-Latif/Abdul-Rahman Shehab (BRN) d. Mohammed Abdulla/Sultan-Khalfan Al Alawi (QAT) 64 62.

Vietnam defeated Sri Lanka 2-1: Harshana Godamanne (SRI) d. Quang-Huy Ngo (VIE) 46 63 63; Minh-Quan Do (VIE) d. Renouk Wijemanne (SRI) 64 64; Minh-Quan Do/Quoc-Khanh Le (VIE) d. Harshana Godamanne/Rajeev Rajapakse (SRI) 63 61.

Play-Off for 1st-4th Positions:

Results carried forward: **Hong Kong, China defeated Malaysia 3-0; Vietnam defeated Sri Lanka 2-1.**

16 July Hong Kong, China defeated Sri Lanka 3-0: Wayne Wong (HKG) d. Harshana Godamanne (SRI) 75 62; Hiu-Tung Yu (HKG) d. Renouk Wijemanne (SRI) 75 62; Brian Hung/ Martin Sayer (HKG) d. Harshana Godamanne/Renouk Wijemanne (SRI) 75 61.

Malaysia defeated Vietnam 3-0: Selvam Veerasingam (MAS) d. Quang-Huy Ngo (VIE) 64 64; Yew-Ming Si (MAS) d. Minh-Quan Do (VIE) 67(9) 64 86; Nikesh Singh Panthlia/Adrian Tan (MAS) d. Minh-Quan Do/Quoc-Khanh Le (VIE) 63 62.

17 July Hong Kong, China defeated Vietnam 3-0: Martin Sayer (HKG) d. Thanh-Hoang Tran (VIE) 63 61; Brian Hung (HKG) d. Minh-Quan Do (VIE) 62 64; Martin Sayer/Hiu-Tung Yu (HKG) d. Minh-Quan Do/Quoc-Khanh Le (VIE) 61 63.

Malaysia defeated Sri Lanka 3-0: Selvam Veerasingam (MAS) d. Harshana Godamanne (SRI) 36 76(5) 75; Yew-Ming Si (MAS) d. Renouk Wijemanne (SRI) 62 61; Nikesh Singh Panthlia/ Adrian Tan (MAS) d. Rajeev Rajapakse/Oshada Wijemanne (SRI) 63 26 97.

Play-off for 5th-8th Positions:

Results carried forward: S**audi Arabia defeated Tajikistan 2-1; Bahrain defeated Qatar 2-1.**

16 July Saudi Arabia defeated Qatar 2-1: Fahad Al Saad (KSA) d. Sultan-Khalfan Al Alawi (QAT) 62 64; Mohammed Abdulla (QAT) d. Omar Al Thagib (KSA) 60 61; Badar Al Megayel/ Fahad Al Saad (KSA) d. Mohammed Abdulla/Sultan-Khalfan Al Alawi (QAT) 06 76(6) 62.

Tajikistan defeated Bahrain 2-1: Abdul-Rahman Shehab (BRN) d. Mansour Yakhyaev (TJK) 67(6) 63 64; Dilshod Sharifi (TJK) d. Khaled Al Thawadi (BRN) 63 63; Dilshod Sharifi/Mirkhusein Yakhyaev (TJK) d. Mohammed Abdul-Latif/Abdul-Rahman Shehab (BRN) 64 64.

17 July Bahrain defeated Saudi Arabia 2-1: Abdul-Rahman Shehab (BRN) d. Badar Al Megayel (KSA) 62 01 ret.;Fahad Al Saad (KSA) d. Khaled Al Thawadi (BRN) 62 36 63; Mohammed Abdul-Latif/Abdul-Rahman Shehab (BRN) d. Badar Al Megayel/Fahad Al Saad (KSA) 75 64.

Qatar defeated Tajikistan 2-1: Mirkhusein Yakhyaev (TJK) d. Abdulla Hajji (QAT) 64 64; Mohammed Abdulla (QAT) d. Dilshod Sharifi (TJK) 75 36 75; Mohammed Abdulla/Sultan-Khalfan Al Alawi (QAT) d. Dilshod Sharifi/Mirkhusein Yakhyaev (TJK) 62 62.

Final Positions: 1. Hong Kong China, 2. Malaysia, 3. Vietnam, 4. Sri Lanka, 5. Bahrain, 6. Saudi Arabia, 7. Qatar, 8. Tajikistan.

Hong Kong China and Malaysia promoted to Asia/Oceania Zone Group II in 2006.
Qatar and Tajikistan relegated to Asia/Oceania Group IV in 2006.

GROUP IV

Europe/Africa Zone

Date: 1-6 March **Venue:** Kampala, Uganda **Surface:** Clay (O)
Group A: Benin, Botswana, Djibouti, Malta, Moldova
Group B: Andorra, Azerbaijan, Mauritius, Rwanda, Senegal, Uganda

Group A

2 March Botswana defeated Benin 2-1: Bokang Setshogo (BOT) d. Romain Setomey (BEN) 62 46 63; Phenyo Matong (BOT) d. Armand Segodo (BEN) 67(12) 60 62; Alphonse Gandonou/ Armand Segodo (BEN) d. Phenyo Matong/Bokang Setshogo (BOT) 62 64.

Moldova defeated Djibouti 3-0: Evghenii Plugiarov (MDA) d. Abdi-Fatah Abdourahman Youssouf (DJI) 60 60; Andrei Ciumac (MDA) d. Kader Mohamed Mogueh (DJI) 60 60; Serghei Cuptov/ Artiom Podgainii (MDA) d. Abdi-Fatah Abdourahaman Youssouf/Kadar Mogueh (DJI) 60 60.

3 March Moldova defeated Malta 3-0: Evghenii Plugariov (MDA) d. Marcus Delicata (MLT) 60 61; Andrei Ciumac (MDA) d. Daniel Ceross (MLT) 62 61; Serghei Cuptov/Artiom Podgainii (MDA) d. Matthew Asciak/Marcus Delicata (MLT) 63 67(5) 61.

Benin defeated Djibouti 3-0: Jean Segodo (BEN) d. Fahim Osman Obsien (DJI) 60 60; Armand Segodo (BEN) d. Kadar Mogueh (DJI) 60 60; Jean Segodo/Romain Setomey (BEN) d. Abdi-Fatah Abdourahman Youssouf/Fahim Osman Obsien (DJI) 60 61.

4 March Moldova defeated Benin 3-0: Evghenii Plugariov (MDA) d. Romain Setomey (BEN) 75 62; Andrei Ciumac (MDA) d. Armand Segodo (BEN) 61 61; Serghei Cuptov/Artiom Podgainii (MDA) d. Alphonse Gandonou/Armand Segodo (BEN) 76(5) 76(5).

Botswana defeated Malta 3-0: Bokang Setshogo (BOT) d. Marcus Delicata (MLT) 62 63; Phenyo Matong (BOT) d. Daniel Ceross (MLT) 36 63 64; Phenyo Matong/Bokang Setshogo (BOT) d. Matthew Asciak/Marcus Delicata (MLT) 36 63 64.

5 March Moldova defeated Botswana 2-1: Evghenii Plugariov (MDA) d. Bokang Setshogo (BOT) 62 64; Andrei Ciumac (MDA) d. Phenyo Matong (BOT) 75 63; Phenyo Matong/Bokang Setshogo (BOT) d. Serghei Cuptov/Artiom Podgainii (MDA) 46 61 63.

Malta defeated Djibouti 3-0: Marcus Delicata (MLT) d. Abdi-Fatah Abdourahman Youssouf (DJI) 61 60; Daniel Ceross (MLT) d. Kader Mogueh (DJI) 61 61; Matthew Asciak/Daniel Ceross (MLT) d. Abdi-Fatah Abdourahman Youssouf/Kadar Mogueh (DJI) 61 61.

6 March Botswana defeated Djibouti 3-0: Bino Rasedisa (BOT) d. Fahim Osman Obsien (DJI) 61 60; Bokang Setshogo (BOT) d. Kadar Mogueh (DJI) 60 60; Bino Rasedisa/Tshepang TIhan Kane (BOT) d. Abdi-Fatah Abdourahman Youssouf/Fahim Osman Obsien (DJI) 63 61.

Benin defeated Malta 3-0: Jean Segodo (BEN) d. Matthew Asciak (MLT) 76(4) 61; Armand Segodo (BEN) d. Daniel Ceross (MLT) 64 64; Jean Segodo/Romain Setomey (BEN) d. Daniel Ceross/Marcus Delicata (MLT) 63 64.

Final Positions: 1. Moldova, 2. Botswana, 3. Benin, 4. Malta, 5. Djibouti.

Moldova and Botswana promoted to Europe/Africa Zone Group III in 2006.

Group B

1 March Azerbaijan defeated Uganda 2-1: Farid Shirinov (AZE) d. Godfrey Uzunga (UGA) 76(6) 75; Patrick Olobo (UGA) d. Fakhraddin Shirinov (AZE) 76(4) 75; Fakhraddin Shirinov/Farid Shirinov (AZE) d. Cedric Babu/Patrick Olobo (UGA) 76(6) 76(2).

Rwanda defeated Senegal 2-1: Jean-Claude Gasigwa (RWA) d. Salif Kante (SEN) 63 76(6); Eric Hagenimana (RWA) d. Youssou Berthe (SEN) 60 63; Youssou Berthe/Salif Kante (SEN) d. Eric Hagenimana/Alain Hakizimana (RWA) 16 63 63.

Andorra defeated Mauritius 3-0: Jean-Baptiste Poux-Gautier (AND) d. Olivier Rey (MRI) 60 61; Paul Gerbaud-Farras (AND) d. Jerome Mamet (MRI) 61 60; Jean-Baptiste Poux-Gautier/ Axel Rabanal (AND) d. Olivier Rey/Mathieu Vallet (MRI) 62 62.

2 March Andorra defeated Rwanda 2-1: Jean-Baptiste Poux-Gautier (AND) d. Jean-Claude Gasigwa (RWA) 61 61; Eric Hagenimana (RWA) d. Paul Gerbaud-Farras (AND) 64 63; Paul Gerbaud-Farras/Jean-Baptiste Poux-Gautier (AND) d. Eric Hagenimana/Alain Hakizimana (RWA) 62 60. Uganda defeated Mauritius 2-1: Godfrey Uzunga (UGA) d. Olivier Rey (MRI) 63 60; Patrick Olobo (UGA) d. Mathieu Vallet (MRI) 60 62; Jerome Mamet/Olivier Rey (MRI) d. James Odongo/Godfrey Uzunga (UGA) 61 46 62.

Senegal defeated Azerbaijan 2-1: Salif Kante (SEN) d. Talat Rahimov (AZE) 75 60; Youssou Berthe (SEN) d. Fakhraddin Shirinov (AZE) 64 16 61; Talat Rahimov/Farid Shirinov (AZE) d. Omar Ka/Mamadou Seye (SEN) 61 64.

3 March Azerbaijan defeated Mauritius 3-0: Farid Shirinov (AZE) d. Mathieu Vallet (MRI) 60 62; Fakhraddin Shirinov (AZE) d. Jerome Mamet (MRI) 63 60; Ramin Hajiyev/Farid Shirinov (AZE) d. Olivier Rey/Mathieu Vallet (MRI) 63 67(3) 75.

Rwanda defeated Uganda 2-1: Godfrey Uzunga (UGA) d. Jean-Claude Gasigwa (RWA) 16 76(5) 55 ret; Eric Hagenimana (RWA) d. Patrick Olobo (UGA) 64 62; Eric Hagenimana/Alain Hakizimana (RWA) d. Cedric Babu/Patrick Olobo (UGA) 60 63.

Andorra defeated Senegal 3-0: Jean-Baptiste Poux-Gautier (AND) d. Salif Kante (SEN) 60 60; Paul Gerbaud-Farras (AND) d. Youssou Berthe (SEN) 61 61; Jean-Baptiste Poux-Gautier/Axel Rabanal (AND) d. Youssou Berthe/Salif Kante (SEN) 64 26 60.

4 March Andorra defeated Azerbaijan 3-0: Jean-Baptiste Poux-Gautier (AND) d. Ramin Hajiyev (AZE) 60 60; Paul Gerbaud-Farras (AND) d. Fakhraddin Shirinov (AZE) 60 60; Paul Gerbaud-Farras/Axel Rabanal (AND) d. Ramin Hajiyev/Talat Rahimov (AZE) 62 62.

Rwanda defeated Mauritius 3-0: Eric Hagenimana (RWA) d. Olivier Rey (MRI) 63 62; Alain Hakizimana (RWA) d. Jerome Mamet (MRI) 60 61; Eric Hagenimana/Alain Hakizimana (RWA) d. Olivier Rey/Mathieu Vallet (MRI) 62 62.

Senegal defeated Uganda 2-1: Salif Kante (SEN) d. James Odongo (UGA) 63 61; Youssou Berthe (SEN) d. Patrick Olobo (UGA) 60 63; Cedric Babu/Patrick Olobo (UGA) d. Youssou Berthe/Salif Kante (SEN) 46 63 64.

5 March Azerbaijan defeated Rwanda 2-1: Farid Shirinov (AZE) d. Jean-Claude Gasigwa (RWA) 64 63; Eric Hagenimana (RWA) d. Fakhraddin Shirinov (AZE) 62 62; Fakhraddin Shirinov/Farid Shirinov (AZE) d. Eric Hagenimana/Alain Hakizimana (RWA) 67(4) 76(6) 63.

Andorra defeated Uganda 3-0: Jean-Baptiste Poux-Gautier (AND) d. James Odongo (UGA) 61 60; Paul Gerbaud-Farras (AND) d. Patrick Olobo (UGA) 60 62; Paul Gerbaud-Farras/Axel Rabanal (AND) d. Cedric Babu/Patrick Olobo (UGA) 63 63.

Senegal defeated Mauritius 2-1: Olivier Rey (MRI) d. Omar Ka (SEN) 60 76(3); Youssou Berthe (SEN) d. Mathieu Vallet (MRI) 61 61; Youssou Berthe/Salif Kante (SEN) d. Jerome Mamet/Olivier Rey (MRI) 62 63.

Final Positions: 1. Andorra, 2. Rwanda, 3. Azerbaijan, 4. Senegal, 5. Uganda, 6. Mauritius.

Andorra and Rwanda promoted to Europe/Africa Zone Group III in 2006.

Americas Zone

Date: 13-17 July **Venue:** San Jose, Costa Rica **Surface:** Hard (O)
Nations: Bermuda, Costa Rica, Trinidad & Tobago, US Virgin Islands

13 July Costa Rica defeated Bermuda 2-1: Janson Bascome (BER) d. Ignasi Roca (CRC) 75 62; Felipe Montenegro (CRC) d. James Collieson (BER) 60 61; Felipe Montenegro/Ignasi Roca (CRC) d. Janson Bascome/Gavin Manders (BER) 63 64.

Trinidad & Tobago defeated Barbados 3-0: Richard Brown (TRI) d. Russell Moseley (BAR) 61 63; Shane Stone (TRI) d. Wkwesi Williams (BAR) 61 61; Shane Stone/Troy Stone (TRI) d. Russell Moseley/Wkwesi Williams (BAR) 62 63.

14 July Bermuda defeated US Virgin Islands 2-1: Janson Bascome (BER) d. Christian Nelthropp (ISV) 62 64; Eugene Highfield (ISV) d. James Collieson (BER) 63 62; Janson Bascome/ Gavin Manders (BER) d. Eugene Highfield/Christian Nelthropp (ISV) 75 46 61.

Barbados defeated Costa Rica 2-1: Wkwesi Williams (BAR) d. Ignasi Roca (CRC) 64 75; Felipe Montenegro (CRC) d. Haydn Lewis (BAR) 46 61 61; Haydn Lewis/Russell Moseley (BAR) d. Felipe Montenegro/Marcos Salazar (CRC) 46 61 62.

15 July Trinidad & Tobago defeated US Virgin Islands 3-0: Richard Brown (TRI) d. Christian Nelthropp (ISV) 60 62; Shane Stone (TRI) d. Eugene Highfield (ISV) 64 76(5); Shane Stone/ Troy Stone (TRI) d. Eugene Highfield/Whitney Mcfarlane (ISV) 36 61 61.

Barbados defeated Bermuda 3-0: Russell Moseley (BAR) d. Janson Bascome (BER) 62 76(3); Haydn Lewis (BAR) d. James Collieson (BER) 76(7) 63; Haydn Lewis/Russell Moseley (BAR) d. Janson Bascome/Gavin Manders (BER) 63 36 63.

16 July Barbados defeated US Virgin Islands 3-0: Russell Moseley (BAR) d. Jereme Cumbermack (ISV) 60 60; Haydn Lewis (BAR) d. Eugene Highfield (ISV) 64 63; Haydn Lewis/ Russell Moseley (BAR) d. Eugene Highfield/Whitney McFarlane (ISV) 62 61.

Costa Rica defeated Trinidad & Tobago 2-1: Richard Brown (TRI) d. Marcos Salazar (CRC) 60 62; Felipe Montenegro (CRC) d. Brent Ching (TRI) 61 64; Felipe Montenegro/Ignasi Roca (CRC) d. Richard Brown/Troy Stone (TRI) 63 62.

17 July Costa Rica defeated US Virgin Islands 3-0: Ignasi Roca (CRC) d. Christian Nelthropp (ISV) 61 62; Felipe Montenegro (CRC) d. Eugene Highfield (ISV) 64 63; Felipe Montenegro/ Ignasi Roca (CRC) d. Whitney McFarlane/Christian Nelthropp (ISV) 64 60.

Trinidad & Tobago defeated Bermuda 3-0: Richard Brown (TRI) d. Gavin Manders (BER) 61 60; Brent Ching (TRI) d. Jenson Bascombe (BER) 62 64; Brent Ching/Troy Stone (TRI) d. James Collieson/Romar Douglas (BER) 63 60.

Final Positions: 1. Trinidad & Tobago, 2. Costa Rica, 3. Barbados, 4. Bermuda, 5. US Virgin Islands.

Costa Rica and Trinidad & Tobago promoted to Americas Zone Group III in 2006.

Asia/Oceania Zone

Date: 27 April-1 May **Venue:** Yangon, Myanmar **Surface:** Hard (O)
Group A: Bangladesh, Kyrgyzstan, Syria, Turkmenistan, United Arab Emirates
Group B: Iraq, Jordan, Myanmar, Oman, Singapore

Group A

27 April United Arab Emirates defeated Turkmenistan 3-0: Mohamed Abdel-Aziz Al Nuaimi (UAE) d. Stanislav Naydyonov (TKM) 61 64; Omar Bahrouzyan (UAE) d. Myalikkuli Mamedkuliyev (TKM) 60 61; Mahmoud-Nader Al Balushi/Omar Bahrouzyan (UAE) d. Dovran Chagylov/Myalikkuli Mamedkuliyev (TKM) 75 64.

Bangladesh defeated Syria 2-1: Lays Salim (SYR) d. Shibu Lal (BAN) 62 46 75; Sree-Amol Roy (BAN) d. Abrahim Ibrahim (SYR) 61 62; Shibu Lal/Sree-Amol Roy (BAN) d. Lays Salim/Yashar Sheet (SYR) 62 76(4).

28 April United Arab Emirates defeated Kyrgyzstan 2-1: Mahmoud-Nader Al Balushi (UAE) d. Ruslan Eshmuhamedov (KGZ) 64 63; Omar Bahrouzyan (UAE) d. Sergey Ni (KGZ) 76(3) 60; Boris Baichorov/Anton Litvinov (KGZ) d. Ghanem Al Hassani/Mohamed Abdel-Aziz Al Nuaimi (UAE) 60 62.

Syria defeated Turkmenistan 3-0: Lays Salim (SYR) d. Stanislav Naydyonov (TKM) 63 61; Abrahim Ibrahim (SYR) d. Myalikkuli Mamedkuliyev (TKM) 62 62; Lays Salim/Yashar Sheet (SYR) d. Dovran Chagylov/Myalikkuli Mamedkuliyev (TKM) 62 62.

29 April Bangladesh defeated United Arab Emirates 2-1: Shibu Lal (BAN) d. Mahmoud-Nader Al Balushi (UAE) 36 65 ret; Sree-Amol Roy (BAN) d. Omar Bahrouzyan (UAE) 61 64; Mohamed Abdel-Aziz Al Nuaimi/Omar Bahrouzyan (UAE) d. Shibu Lal/Sree-Amol Roy (BAN) 63 26 63.

Kyrgyzstan defeated Turkmenistan 3-0: Boris Baichorov (KGZ) d. Dovran Chagylov (TKM) 62 63; Sergey Ni (KGZ) d. Myalikkuli Mamedkuliyev (TKM) 75 60; Ruslan Eshmuhamedov/ Anton Litvinov (KGZ) d. Dovran Chagylov/Myalikkuli Mamedkuliyev (TKM) 75 61.

30 April Syria defeated Kyrgyzstan 3-0: Lays Salim (SYR) d. Boris Baichorov (KGZ) 36 61 61; Abrahim Ibrahim (SYR) d. Sergey Ni (KGZ) 64 75; Hayan Maarouf/Yashar Sheet (SYR) d. Boris Baichorov/Anton Litvinov (KGZ) 76(4) 76(3).

Bangladesh defeated Turkmenistan 2-1: Shibu Lal (BAN) d. Stanislav Naydyonov (TKM) 61 60; Sree-Amol Roy (BAN) d. Myalikkuli Mamedkuliyev (TKM) 61 62; Dovran Chagylov/ Myalikkuli Mamedkuliyev (TKM) d. Alamgir Hossain/Dipu Lal (BAN) 57 63 64.

1 May United Arab Emirates defeated Syria 2-1: Mohamed Abdel-Aziz Al Nuaimi (UAE) d. Lays Salim (SYR) 75 67(7) 63; Omar Bahrouzyan (UAE) d. Abrahim Ibrahim (SYR) 61 62; Hayan Maarouf/Yashar Sheet (SYR) d. Mohamed Abdel-Aziz Al Nuaimi/Omar Bahrouzyan (UAE) 36 63 62.

Bangladesh defeated Kyrgyzstan 3-0: Shibu Lal (BAN) d. Anton Litvinov (KGZ) 63 64; Sree-Amol Roy (BAN) d. Sergey Ni (KGZ) 61 63; Alamgir Hossain/Shibu Lal (BAN) d. Anton Litvinov/Sergey Ni (KGZ) 63 67(5) 64.

Final Positions: 1. Bangladesh, 2. United Arab Emirates, 3. Syria, 4. Kyrgyzstan, 5. Turkmenistan.

Bangladesh promoted to Asia/Oceania Zone Group III in 2006.

Group B

27 April Oman defeated Myanmar 3-0: Mohammed Al Nabhani (OMA) d. Zaw-Zaw Latt (MYA) 67(4) 42 ret.; Khalid Al Nabhani (OMA) d. Mg Tu Maw (MYA) 67(5) 75 60; Khalid Al Nabhani/Mohammed Al Nabhani (OMA) d. Min Min/Hla Win Naing (MYA) 75 62.

Singapore defeated Iraq 3-0: Kok-Huen Kam (SIN) d. Akram Al Karem (IRQ) 63 62; Stanley Armando (SIN) d. Nasir Hatam (IRQ) 61 36 62; Daniel Dewandaka/Ming-Chye Lim (SIN) d. Akram Al Karem/Hussain Rasheed (IRQ) 61 62.

28 April Oman defeated Jordan 3-0: Mohammed Al Nabhani (OMA) d. Ahmad Al Hadid (JOR) 62 62; Khalid Al Nabhani (OMA) d. Tareq Talal Shkakwa (JOR) 62 63; Khalid Al Nabhani/ Mohammed Al Nabhani (OMA) d. Mohammed Al Hadid/Ahmad Tbayshat (JOR) 62 62.

Singapore defeated Myanmar 3-0: Kok-Huen Kam (SIN) d. Min Min (MYA) 75 64; Stanley Armando (SIN) d. Mg Tu Maw (MYA) 75 75; Daniel Dewandaka/Ming-Chye Lim (SIN) d. Zaw-Zaw Latt/Mg Tu Maw (MYA) 46 62 64.

29 April Oman defeated Iraq 3-0: Mohammed Al Nabhani (OMA) d. Akram Al Karem (IRQ) 75 63; Khalid Al Nabhani (OMA) d. Nasir Hatam (IRQ) 62 76(8); Khalid Al Nabhani/Mohammed Al Nabhani (OMA) d. Akram Al Karem/Hussain Rasheed (IRQ) 63 63.

Myanmar defeated Jordan 3-0: Zaw-Zaw Latt (MYA) d. Ahmad Al Hadid (JOR) 76(2) 60; Mg Tu Maw (MYA) d. Tareq Talal Shkakwa (JOR) 63 75; Min Min/Hla Win Naing (MYA) d. Mohammed Al Hadid/Ahmad Tbayshat (JOR) 62 46 63.

30 April Singapore defeated Jordan 2-1: Ahmad Al Hadid (JOR) d. Kok-Huen Kam (SIN) 64 76(5); Stanley Armando (SIN) d. Tareq Talal Shkakwa (JOR) 62 63; Daniel Dewandaka/ Ming-Chye Lim (SIN) d. Ahmad Al Hadid/Tareq Talal Shkakwa (JOR) 60 61.

Myanmar defeated Iraq 3-0: Zaw-Zaw Latt (MYA) d. Hussain Rasheed (IRQ) 61 60; Mg Tu Maw (MYA) d. Nasir Hatam (IRQ) 62 63; Min Min/Hla Win Naing (MYA) d. Nasir Hatam/Hussain Rasheed (IRQ) 63 76(6)

1 May Singapore defeated Oman 2-1: Daniel Dewandaka (SIN) d. Mohammed Al Nabhani (OMA) 64 64; Khalid Al Nabhani (OMA) d. Stanley Armando (SIN) 75 63; Stanley Armando/ Daniel Dewandaka (SIN) d. Khalid Al Nabhani/Mohammed Al Nabhani (OMA) 62 26 75.

Jordan defeated Iraq 3-0: Ahmad Al Hadid (JOR) d. Akram AL Karem (IRQ) 63 62; Tareq Talal Shkakwa (JOR) d. Nasir Hatam (IRQ) 63 61; Mohammed Al Hadid/Ahmad Tbayshat (JOR) d. Hussain A Rasheed/Mohammed Salman (IRQ) 61 67(3) 62.

Final Positions: 1. Singapore, 2. Oman, 3. Myanmar, 4. Jordan, 5. Iraq.

Singapore promoted to Asia/Oceania Zone Group III in 2006.

ACKNOWLEDGMENTS

SOME PEOPLE SUGGESTED TO me at various times in 2005 that I was unlucky to be writing the Davis Cup "Year in Tennis" in a season in which so many fancied names fell so early. I enjoyed correcting them. Not only am I a history graduate who particularly enjoyed Russian and German history with all its impacts on central and eastern Europe, but part of my family hails from central Europe. I was in Berlin as a tourist either side of the Wall falling, and watched with jaw-dropping fascination from my vantage point at the BBC in London how the momentous crumbling of the eastern bloc took place in the latter months of 1989. For me to be able to write the Davis Cup book in a year whose exploits were so firmly rooted in the aftermath of the 1989-93 redrawing of the European map has been a pure pleasure, and I hope I have done it justice.

In addition, my father came to England as a refugee at the age of 12. I can't claim to have an empathetic understanding of what being a refugee means, but I'm aware of many of the spin-offs, good and bad. As a result, it was a source of great satisfaction for me to be able to document a year in which the dominant player was a man who also left his country at 12 to pick up the pieces in another land. I only revealed my dad's past to Ivan Ljubicic after the Final, but all year I felt a sort of "connection" with Croatia's hero, and feel particularly proud that one of tennis's polyglots has become a national hero with the dignity to recognise that he's also a citizen of the world.

Because I can only be in one place at a time, I am eternally grateful to others who have been my eyes and ears in 2005. In alphabetical order they are: Nicola Arzani, John Barrett, Alfredo Bernardi, Neven Berticevic, Philippe Bouin, Guillermo Caporaletti, Andre Christopher, Richard Eaton, Craig Gabriel, David Law, John Lindsay, Ivan Ljubicic, Paul-Henri Mathieu, Daniel Monnin, Andrei Pavel, Gregor Sket, René Stauffer, Tom Tebbutt, Rodrigo Valdebenito, and Zuzana Wisterova.

Special thanks go to Barbara Travers and her staff at the ITF Communications department, in particular Andrew Rigby who has been the most encouraging of editors and turned me into an American—at least in spelling! Once again Sharon Smith at Domino 4 has done a fine job on the layout.

Finally, thanks and a big hug go to the two women in my life, my partner Louise and my daughter Tamara. At four, Tamara is now old enough to miss me when I go away, so a copy of this book is reserved for her in the hope that one day she'll understand that some of my absences from home really were worthwhile.

Chris Bowers

PHOTOGRAPHY CREDITS

- Ian Burrows: 51 (top)
- Sergio Carmona: 24, 25, 26, 27, 28, 64 (bottom left), 65 (bottom right), 80 (bottom right upper), 86, 87, 103
- Antoine Couvercelle: 50 (top), 60, 61, 62, 63, 81 (bottom right), 101 (top left upper)
- Philippe Crochet: 92, 93, 101 (top left lower), 116 (top right), 117 (bottom left upper)
- Corinne Dubreuil: 33, 34, 35, 44 (top right), 45 (top left and bottom right), 65 (top left and top right), 81 (top right lower)
- Arne Forsell: 64 (upper top left), 80 (top right), 94, 95
- GEPA: 80 (top left lower), 96, 100 (bottom left)
- Robert Ghement: 21, 22, 23
- Manuel Gonzalez: 84/85, 98, 99
- Tommy Hindley: 81 (bottom left upper), 90, 91, 117 (bottom middle)
- Henk Koster: 29, 30, 31, 32, 44 (top left and bottom left), 54, 55, 64 (bottom right), 65 (bottom left), 81 (top left), 83
- Davor Kovacevic: 10 (bottom), 114 (top)
- Sergio Llamera: 12/13, 39, 40, 41, 44 (bottom right), 64 (lower top left), 81 (bottom left lower), 116 (top left), 117 (top left),
- Susan Mullane: 14, 15, 16, 17, 18, 19, 20, 45 (upper bottom left), 47, 64 (top middle) 80 (top left upper), 100 (bottom right), 101 (top right, bottom right upper, bottom left)
- Jeremy Piper: 42, 43
- Tomas Purwin/Paul Zimmer: 88, 89, 100 (top left)
- Reuters: 48/49, 50 (middle and bottom), 51 (middle and bottom), 52, 53, 56, 57, 58, 59, 64 (top right), 67, 68/69, 70 (top), 71, 72, 73, 74, 80 (bottom right lower)
- Ron Turenne: 97
- Paul Zimmer: 36, 37, 38, 45 (top right and lower bottom left), 65 (bottom middle), 70 (bottom), 75, 76, 77, 78, 79, 80 (bottom left), 81 (top right upper), 100 (top right), 101 (bottom right lower), 116 (bottom right), 117 (top right),
- Paul Zimmer/Daniel Maurer: Cover (front and back), inside cover, 6, 9, 10 (top), 104-5, 106, 107, 108, 109, 110, 111, 112, 113, 114 (bottom), 115, 116 (bottom left), 117 (bottom left lower, bottom right) 119